Praise for *The Lightmaker's Manifesto*

"We yearn for more joy in our lives. We feel called to change the world. But we struggle because joy and activism feel so separate and, sometimes, even mutually exclusive. Karen Walrond offers us a completely different path—an integrated and intentional approach to life that ignites and fuels both our joy and our ability to make change. I can't stop thinking about joy-fueled activism and Karen's ability to shine her light so we can find our own."

—Brené Brown, PhD, author of the *New York Times* #1 bestseller *Dare to Lead*

"*The Lightmaker's Manifesto* is essential reading for all those determined to change the world without sacrificing their humanity and joy. Karen Walrond's writing shimmers with wisdom, truth, and light."

—Glennon Doyle, author of the *New York Times* #1 bestseller *Untamed*

"Tired. Stressed. Overwhelmed. These are the words that often accompany the change-makers and justice-seekers in the world. But in *The Lightmaker's Manifesto*, Walrond graciously invites us to connect our work to a deeply abiding joy."

—Austin Channing Brown, author of *New York Times* bestseller *I'm Still Here: Black Dignity in a World Made for Whiteness*

"Karen Walrond's wondrous book *The Lightmaker's Manifesto* is an inspired guide for those who want to learn to prioritize joy. Walrond shares personal stories, profiles of lightmakers, and specific activities to help you move toward joy. We all need a copy of this book."

—Shauna M. Ahern, author of *Enough: Notes From a Woman Who Has Finally Found It* and James Beard Award–winning cookbooks, and founder of Finding Your Joy

"More intimate than one-size-fits-all self-help and more expansive than a memoir, this is a practical and inspirational guide to help each of us discover how we can create more light: light by which to navigate a nervous world, illuminate next steps, and heal the world in tiny and global, personal and sweeping ways. *The Lightmaker's Manifesto* is precisely the book so many of us have been waiting for."
—Cathleen Falsani, journalist and author of *The God Factor* and *Sin Boldly: A Field Guide for Grace*

"At Amy Poehler's Smart Girls, we have a simple motto: 'Change the world by being yourself.' However, because trying to change the world, even in a small way, is tough work, and being yourself isn't always easy, we often feel disappointed and joyless. We don't experience the great joy in just being alive, or remember that joy comes in the midst of disappointment, not instead of it. Karen Walrond has grasped this deep truth, and she invites us to see what we have so often been missing. *The Lightmaker's Manifesto* offers all of us a way to look at a broken world, and at our incomplete selves, with a fresh and vital perspective."
—Meredith Walker, producer and cofounder of Amy Poehler's Smart Girls

"Karen Walrond shares life lessons that will compel you to go back and pick up the parts of you that were sacrificed in order to serve. This book reminds you that you're not alone in your experiences and you're going to be okay."
—Romal Tune, author of *Love Is an Inside Job: Getting Vulnerable with God*

THE
LIGHTMAKER'S
MANIFESTO

THE
LIGHTMAKER'S
MANIFESTO

HOW TO WORK FOR CHANGE
WITHOUT LOSING
YOUR JOY

KAREN WALROND

Broadleaf Books
Minneapolis

Cover design: Gearbox Studio

Print ISBN: 978-1-5064-6994-2
eBook ISBN: 978-1-5064-6995-9

Printed in Canada

For Alexis

CONTENTS

CONTENTS

PART IV: FIRE AND LIGHT

PART I
CLEARING

We knew, without a doubt, that lighting a fire was the most important thing to do. We needed to bring the group together and provide a sense of home in the appalling circumstances in which we found ourselves. But how?

—Daniel Hume, *Fire Making: The Forgotten Art of Conjuring Flame with Spark, Tinder, and Skill*

One of the greatest things you have in life is that no one has the authority to tell you what you want to be. You're the one who'll decide what you want to be.

—Jaime Escalante

1 | ON LIFE-CHANGERS AND LIGHTMAKERS

We arrived in Nairobi late in the evening and made a beeline for our hotel to get some rest. I was exhausted and disheveled: I'm no stranger to international flights, but a continuous twenty-four-hour stretch of travel is no joke. Still, I knew this trip would be worth it.

I was visiting Kenya with a group of journalists and bloggers at the invitation of the ONE Campaign. Founded by Bono, the front man of the internationally renowned rock band U2, ONE is a nonpartisan advocacy organization dedicated to the fight against extreme poverty and preventable disease, particularly in Africa. The purpose of our trip was to share firsthand accounts of what we witnessed, in the hopes that with our stories of the progress being made in Kenya, we would inspire the readers of our words (and in my case, the viewers of my photographs) to join in the fight against poverty. As you might imagine, I was thrilled to be on this expedition: while I had visited Africa before, this was my first trip to this region, fulfilling a lifelong dream of finally seeing the bustling city of Nairobi with my own eyes.

That dream would have to wait for a few days. At dawn the next morning, our jetlagged group made its way back to Jomo Kenyatta International Airport to take an early domestic flight to Kisumu,

Kenya's third largest city, on the shores of Lake Victoria. Although I didn't know it at the time, Kisumu, and its surrounding Nyanza province, was ground zero when it comes to infectious diseases: HIV, tuberculosis, and malaria, among others, were common in the region, and the highest prevalence of those diseases in Kenya was in this area. Nyanza province also happens to be one of the poorest places in the country.

Our mission was to witness the work that the Kenya Medical Research Institute (KEMRI), the scientific research arm of Kenya's Ministry of Health, was doing in collaboration with the US Centers for Disease Control and Prevention (CDC). Our flight landed and we boarded a bus for the quick drive to the site, where we split up into groups of two to shadow HIV home healthcare workers. These dedicated folks were KEMRI's representatives who traveled throughout the countryside, testing families for HIV and counseling them on how to reduce the spread of the disease. Because many of the families in the region live in relatively remote rural areas, it was difficult (not to mention discouraging) for them to travel the long distances on foot to get to the clinics to determine their status. So instead, KEMRI and the CDC came to them.

My travel companion for the day was Amy, a young journalist from San Francisco, and we were quickly paired with two Kenyan healthcare counselors who were consummate professionals: Sam, a jovial and passionate young man with twinkling eyes and a great smile, and Grace, his more reserved, no-nonsense counterpart. After they briefed us on what we were about to experience, we set off.

It was a sunny day, and the red ochre path was bright under the vivid blue sky. I fell in step with Sam, who was carrying a large, sealed plastic crate filled with testing equipment on one shoulder. We talked about how he became interested in home healthcare testing.

"Do you like your job?" I asked.

He grinned, and his eyes seemed to sparkle even more. "Oh yes, definitely."

"Yeah?" I asked, "What's the best part?"

"Managing other counselors."

I was taken aback. I hadn't understood that there was a hierarchy within the home healthcare program, nor did I realize that Sam was Grace's boss. "Really? How many do you manage?"

"Eight. I love it. I love helping them give a great service to our clients. I hope one day that I can run a program like this in other parts of Kenya."

We continued along the path through the tall grasses before at last arriving at a clearing with a small house made of rust-colored mud walls and an intricately thatched roof. "This is the family," Sam said, introducing us to a father, a mother, and their two small children. They invited us inside their home.

Once we got situated, Sam made more formal introductions of Amy and me. He explained to us that the family knew we would be visiting their home that day and had given their consent to our writing and publishing what we witnessed. He also assured us that the family already knew their status, having been tested about a month earlier, and that they were willing to undergo the test again so we could see exactly how the procedure was done. Grace would conduct the testing and counseling session in Swahili, and Sam would act as our translator.

Then Grace got to work. She covered a little table with a sterile cloth and set up her equipment. The test consisted of a pin prick on the index finger, where a small amount of blood was collected and placed on two test strips (for double-checking purposes). The test only took about fifteen minutes and was similar to a pregnancy test: if one line appeared on the strip, the test was negative, and if two lines appeared, the test was positive. In situations such as this one, where the mother tested positive, the workers conducted further tests on the children, with the consent of their parents.

Once the family knew their status, they were counseled on ways to protect themselves. In the case of this family, Grace described the precautions the couple needed to take to ensure that the mother didn't infect the father, who had tested negative. The parents were given condoms and, with wooden models, shown how to use them. Finally, the members of the family who had tested positive were given referrals to a clinic where they could receive free medications from the Ministry of Health.

The results of this initiative were impressive. In the previous twelve months, this home healthcare program had recruited and trained 150 counselors who go door-to-door to provide this type of counseling, testing, and household education. Further, the United States Agency for International Development provided care packages for each family in the program: a jerry can for collecting water in a nearby river, a cloth to strain the collected water and drops to purify it, and mosquito nets to help prevent malaria. (Malaria poses a huge and deadly risk to those who test HIV-positive, given their suppressed immune systems.) In that year alone, 130,000 people had been counseled and tested, and there was an 85 percent acceptance rate for the services. In addition, 50 percent of those testing positive sought care and treatment.

During the preceding month, after the family we were visiting had officially learned of their status, they had taken Sam and Grace's counsel to heart and had already begun to receive treatment. This quick, easy test had enabled the family to take the necessary steps to ensure that all members could live full, productive lives.

After Grace finished her work, the father wanted to take us on a tour of their property. He showed us his verdant kitchen garden, lush with corn and other produce to feed his family. He led us on a ten-minute hike to show us the river where his family collected the water they used for drinking and washing. As we walked, I caught up with Grace and complimented her on her professionalism.

"You're really great, Grace," I said.

"Thanks," she replied quietly, seriously.

"Do you enjoy your job?" I asked.

At this, her face broke into a wide smile—the first I'd seen since we met. "I *really* do," she said enthusiastically. "I mean, why wouldn't I? I'm a life-changer!"

◆ ◆ ◆

Watching Sam and Grace work at that little homestead in rural Nyanza, I couldn't help but be impressed by their commitment to social good. In the course of their efforts, Grace and Sam clearly witness difficult things. They see close up the aching realities of poverty and illness and death. Their work is tiring, and given that they do it all on foot, very slow. Still, there is no denying the joy with which they serve their community. Sam's twinkling eyes, Grace's sudden, unfettered smile: these are testaments to this joy, which, frankly, confused me. How was it possible that the labor of alleviating suffering or working for justice could inspire contentment, or even joy? Can life-changers keep facing all that is wrong with the world—over and over and over again—without burning out? Could advocacy fuel joy—and vice versa?

Most images of activism that we see in the media don't exactly inspire feelings of joy: a lone man putting his life on the line by blocking the path of a column of military tanks in Tiananmen Square, say. Or gaunt ascetics enduring lengthy and excruciating hunger strikes. Protestors being brutalized by police dogs, fire hoses, and tear gas. The people in these situations, while undeniably powerful and courageous, aren't exactly *joyful-looking*. These images illustrate the bravery and resoluteness of the human spirit, but they can also intimidate anyone looking for their own path to changing the world for the better. "If *that's* what it takes to change the world," we think, "I'm not sure I'm the right person. I have a job/family/partner who depends on me. I care, but I can't put my life on the line."

Trust me: I resonate deeply with this thinking. In my not-so-distant past, I had come up with a pretty extensive list of reasons why an activist life wasn't for me. For starters, my own description of the word *activism* came fairly close to the *Merriam-Webster* dictionary definition: "a doctrine or practice that emphasizes direct vigorous action especially in support of or opposition to one side of a controversial issue."

Vigorous action: I'm sorry, but that sounds *really* uncomfortable. I mean, I'd participated in the odd family-friendly women's march or Pride parade in my day, but I had never really been a part of "vigorous action": something where my physical safety or freedom was truly and imminently threatened. That kind of behavior was for other folks.

And even if vigorous action *was* my jam, the truth is I was just too busy. With all the time it took going to work, taking care of family members, doing odd jobs around the house, taking the car to the mechanic, attending weekly church services, going to the gym . . . when, exactly, was I supposed to be an activist? It was about all I could do to remember to toss things in the recycling bin. The idea of letter-writing or marching on top of my regular day-to-day life was just too exhausting to contemplate—and I don't care how joyful anyone made it sound. Surely activism was the purview of young, single people, with no responsibilities and tons of energy. Let the youth handle it.

Third, what if I said the wrong thing? I mean, especially in areas of activism like human rights or racial equity or LGBTQ+ justice, it can take a while to understand all the underlying issues affecting each community. Despite all my best intentions, it seemed that the risk of saying the wrong thing—and accidentally offending the very people for whom I was ostensibly advocating—was *really* high. And let's be honest: in our world of social media and other highly visible forms of personal expression, that mistake may come with some painfully public consequences and lessons learned. Surely the only way to protect my joy was to stay out of activism altogether.

Besides, the decision to pursue activism or advocacy, whether as vocation or avocation, is a daunting one. The ills of the world are so numerous that it can be hard to choose what issue to tackle. There's climate change. Women's rights issues. LGBTQ+ discrimination. Child labor crimes. Female genital mutilation. Domestic violence. Child abuse. Endangered species. Universally accessible health care. Rights for people with disabilities. Fighting for democracy. Fighting against religious persecution.

And that's just off the top of my head.

So believe me, I get it: I've wrestled with every one of these thoughts. As will become apparent in the coming pages, it took me an astonishing amount of time to consider myself an activist. But over time, I would find myself volunteering at a small event, or attending a tiny fundraiser, or going to a protest. Little by little, I've learned that despite all the conceivable downsides, doing this work is strongly weighted toward the upsides. Activism can creep up on you. Then suddenly, if you're lucky, you find advocacy has become a fulfilling part of your life.

And it turns out I'd been an activist for longer than I'd realized.

◆ ◆ ◆

For most of my adulthood, I had lived a safe, comfortable life, making my career in solid, technical fields. First, I was a structural engineer for a construction company that built refineries; later, I was a lawyer in the software and energy industries. It was a good living, but to balance the eight to ten hours each day that I was using my analytical brain, I took up photography. I had never intended photography to be anything more than a hobby—a chance to exercise some creativity. I'd spent my entire life believing I wasn't creative, but I figured that photography, with its ISO numbers and f-stops, would be sufficiently analytical for my logical brain to grasp. (It wasn't until much later on that it occurred to me that the Latin root of the word *photography* literally means to "draw with light." If there was ever a more artistic-sounding definition, I don't know what it is.)

So as I approached the end of law school, on a whim I convinced a fashion photographer friend of mine, Josef, to take me camera shopping and show me the ropes. Bless him, he did, and my first big purchase was an ancient, secondhand single-lens-reflex Nikon film camera and an even older 50mm lens. Josef took me around town for one day, encouraging me to shoot rolls and rolls of film while he pointed out a few features of my new-to-me machine. Then I was completely on my own—and my love for photography was officially ignited. I began shooting constantly, taking my camera with me on business trips, ensuring that I booked a few hours to myself to explore each destination through my lens.

Time passed, and when I eventually stopped practicing law altogether, I knew that whatever work that followed would have to involve photography. By then I had been shooting for almost twenty years, and had even coauthored a book on how to make expressive, narrative photographs. But I still didn't have any idea how my photography might fuel my work.

As a lawyer, I had done a lot of work in diversity, equity, and inclusion, for which I'd developed a passion. (Admittedly, this passion was probably inevitable for an Afro-Caribbean immigrant from Trinidad and Tobago, who had navigated the considerably white world of the corporate energy industry for years.) I decided to combine this deep interest in inclusion and belonging with my love of photography and wrote and shot my first book, *The Beauty of Different: Observations of a Confident Misfit*. The book was a compilation of stories and interviews of people from all walks of life who had taken their gifts (and sometimes their perceived flaws) and used them to thrive.

The book did well, as books go, but more meaningful for me than sales was the process of actually creating the text and images. Conducting the interviews, photographing the subjects, and sharing their stories awoke in me a deep desire—a personal mission, in fact—to do whatever I could to counter discrimination and bigotry of all forms. Sharing photographs and stories of people vulnerable enough to give me a glimpse of their uncommon beauty became a passion. I shared these images and stories in my book, on my website, and on stages in front of audiences of thousands. I encouraged people to join me in telling their own stories and sharing their images. Doing so, I maintained, would result in resonance. It would help create community. And together, we'd create light.

One day, someone mentioned my work to the ONE Campaign. They contacted me and the next thing I knew, I was applying for a travel visa to Kenya. That journey to Kenya—the one where I met Sam and Grace—was the first of several trips to Africa over the next few years, the result of what became a deeply fulfilling relationship with ONE. That first call felt very much like it occurred by happenstance, but in hindsight, I realize that it was actually a natural evolution of my work. Using the skills I'd acquired while learning photography and which had brought me joy—gifts that involved *drawing with light*—allowed me to serve in ways I could not have imagined when I was practicing law, even if I had tried. The fact that my advocacy and service filled my own life with joy and light was the icing on the cake.

While I don't travel nearly as much as I used to, my work is underpinned by an ongoing desire to fight discrimination and foster interconnectedness through the sharing of stories and images of beauty. This desire has been bolstered by a commitment to working with diverse organizations—as well as people of all races, abilities, ages, sexual orientations, and gender identities—from every corner of the world who are determined to make a difference in their communities. And when I say "underpinned," I mean that at this point, this mission invades every waking moment of my day. It guides almost every decision I make.

So while it took me a moment before I knew myself to be an activist, over time, I now know that the *Merriam-Webster* definition of *activism* is too narrow. It's similar to the way that, when some people hear the word *attorney*, they only imagine a criminal prosecutor—certainly accurate, but failing to encompass all the other forms that being an attorney can take. For sure, God bless the activists who risk life and limb for their causes. Thanks to their selfless efforts, many unjust laws have been changed and many civil rights have been won.

But when I think of all the ways activists can show up, I'm reminded of a reflection my friend, author Erin Loechner, shared about the Christmas story—specifically, about the innkeeper who offered a stable to a young, pregnant family unable to find any lodging. Erin wrote, "I'm thinking less about the wisemen who traveled from afar toting riches and gifts, and I'm thinking more about the innkeeper. The one who quietly served those nearest, day in and day out, and who—in the end—stretched out a bit of creativity to make room for something altogether lovely."

This is it, exactly: we often forget the people who quietly and diligently work behind those turbulent scenes for good and justice— those who daily activate their own gifts and talents and determination as part of a larger cause. Those folks, in my thinking, deserve to be called "activists" too. After all, the root word of *activist* is the Latin word *actus*, meaning "a doing, a driving force, or an impulse." Measured, committed, value-driven actions, executed with determination on behalf of others: these can change the world too.

The novelist Edith Wharton once said, "There are two ways of spreading light: to be the candle or the mirror that reflects it." I've always loved this quotation and took it to mean that you could either *be* the light—simply by having a loving or caring nature, or demeanor, or outlook on life—or you could *reflect* the light, by treating those who were good and kind to you with equal or even greater magnanimity. Yet over time, I've come to believe that Wharton's words omit a third way to spread light, and that is to *make* it. More than simply defaulting to kindness, or waiting for an act of generosity to respond in kind, we can proactively take the things that fuel us—our gifts and our passions—and use them to serve the world. We're called to activate others and advocate for the causes that mean the most to us.

We can take inspiration from Grace, the home healthcare worker in Kisumu. Grace wasn't content to simply be pleasant or return the kindnesses others extended to her—in other words, simply be a candle or a mirror. Instead, armed with the knowledge that her community was being ravaged by the HIV epidemic, she purposefully gained education and training to help make a difference.

She travels all over her community using those skills to ensure that those who are impoverished have the same access to healthcare as those who might have more money and access. As part of her work, she witnesses injustice, faces painful situations, and has difficult conversations, like informing a young mother that she is HIV positive. And yet she clearly loves what she does. Talking about her work prompts an instinctive and unbridled smile, without hesitation. Her work creates light not only in the lives of the people she helps, but also in her own life.

Grace calls herself a life-changer. And she is. But by using her skills, education, and passion to help others in ways that bring her joy, she is also a *lightmaker*.

And if light can be made, it can be practiced. We can mindfully identify and call on the gifts and skills and experiences that we already have—the talents and traits that already bring joy to our lives, the things that "light us up"—and ritualize them. We can use them in ways that serve the world while simultaneously helping us to maintain our determination, cultivate resilience, and even tend to our own spirits. And by being purposeful in using our gifts and talents as fuel for our commitment to serve, even in a world of tremendous pain and injustice, we can minimize the possibility of burnout—or even avoid it altogether.

This isn't to say that lightmaking is *easy*. Pursuing a life of activism in a way that inspires joy requires a considerable amount of introspection and forethought. There's planning involved. In fact, the process is similar to the methods an experienced backpacker might use to build a campfire. First, she would create a clearing. Then she would look for appropriate tinder—fuel to easily begin her fire. She would create a spark to ignite the tinder, and then nurture the flame to create fire and light. Similarly, becoming the type of activist whose work is inextricably linked to joy requires mindfulness, and

intention, and clarity about what brings your life meaning and purpose and space to identify your own innate skills—your "tinder."
Once you've taken steps toward your activism, you'll need tools to
nurture your inner call to serve—your *soulfire*, you might call it—
to make light in the world and for yourself.

In the pages of this book, I'll share just how to do that. I'll
introduce you to other lightmakers: luminaries whose passions are
wildly diverse, from political activism to antidiscrimination work,
from women's rights to criminal justice reform. The people you'll
meet in these pages generously share wisdom and stories from
their own advocacy journeys. For example, Sikh American advocate Valarie Kaur describes how she listens to her own inner wise
woman to establish longevity in her labor for social justice. Tarana
Burke, founder of the Me Too movement, shares how her personal
tribe—her "star collective"—provides the compassion and community needed to tend her spirit when things get difficult. Researcher
and storyteller Brené Brown shares how she taps into her values and
her courage to do the right thing, even when it's terrifying to do so.
And psychologist Sean Fitzpatrick and pastor Aaron Billard provide
insights into the ways in which activism might actually be so meaningful as to feel spiritual, even transcendent.

And that's just for starters.

These folks exemplify the most critical insight I've gained in my
own life as an activist: that there's no one way to change the world.
The world changes when we take inspiration from all the different forms of good work and light and make them our own. So I'll
invite you to take the stories you encounter in these pages, consider them, and use what's useful. Experiment with the advice and
counsel that you read. Read the sections in the back of the book—
"The Lightmaker's Manifesto" and the exercises in "The Lightmaker's Manual"—and make them your own. The manifesto offers

a statement of purpose for lightmakers that you can adopt or adapt for your use. The manual offers prompts, exercises, and templates for cultivating a joyful, light-filled life of activism. As you encounter these resources, twist them, turn them, and allow them to morph into what works best for your life, your passions, and your cause.

And with that, let's make some light.

2 | ON JOY, MEANING, AND SURVIVING A HURRICANE

There's a reason it's possible for joy to live in concert with activism, and to do so far more naturally than happiness can. Happiness is a fleeting, pleasurable emotion caused by external circumstances. You're happy when someone remembers your birthday. Or when the barista puts extra whipped cream on your hot chocolate. Or when it's payday. Happiness occurs in the moment, as an immediate reaction to an event, and it can fade just as quickly away. Happiness is transient.

Joy, on the other hand, is something more profound and long-lasting. Often, joy finds itself rooted in much deeper things, like meaning and purpose. And joy can, paradoxically, arise directly out of sadness and pain and loss.

In the late summer of 2017, our family was given a profound lesson in this paradox. Then, as now, my family and I were living in Houston, Texas. Houston lies squarely in Hurricane Alley: the area of warm water that begins on the western coast of Africa, stretches all the way across the Atlantic, and ends at the Gulf Coast of the United States. Hurricanes are simply a fact of life when you live in Houston. So as Hurricane Harvey approached the Texas Gulf Coast, while we were all alarmed, we weren't entirely surprised. The forecast indicated Harvey would make landfall about 150 miles south of us; dangerous winds were unlikely, but projected rain amounts were concerning.

Houston is no stranger to flooding, and in prior recent years our city had experienced a few severe floods in which many people lost their homes—and those losses were simply from unusually enthusiastic rainstorms, not hurricanes. But even in those previous events, our own area streets had remained bone dry. Our neighborhood wasn't—and still isn't—in a flood zone. So evacuation seemed like an overreaction. In fact, even though I'd let our flood insurance lapse a few years earlier, I was barely concerned.

Turns out some concern was warranted.

The storm made landfall and turned toward Houston, dropping an apocalyptic amount of rain in its wake. For the first time in ten years, water began to seep into our home, under the doorways, and even up through the floorboards. We quickly evacuated our daughter, Alexis, to her best friend's house, but my husband, Marcus, and I decided to stay, hoping to forestall any damage. By the next day, however, it was apparent that we also needed to leave. The levees in our neighborhood were failing, and the murky water in our home was starting to be measured in feet rather than inches. Marcus and I made a plan: we would wade to a dryer area where roads were passable and Alex's friend's father, Dustin, could pick us up.

And so we set off: clad in old jeans and tees and raincoats we had managed to salvage, Marcus carried a few days' clothing in a waterproof backpack and our trembling sixteen-pound dog, Soca, in his arms. It took only seconds before we were all soaked through. When we approached the intersection where we had planned to cross the nearby bayou, we blanched: the water had broken its banks. The sleepy little creek that normally meandered alongside our neighbor-hood hike-and-bike trail was now a swollen, raging river. Wading through would have been a challenge at best, deadly at worst.

"I don't care," I told Marcus, as the tropical storm-level winds whipped around us and the rain pelted down. *"We have to get to our kid."*

Marcus knows better than to argue with me when I get like this, so we grabbed hold of each other to steady ourselves and started wading in. As the water got deeper, I began to think twice about what we were about to do. *This is insane,* I whispered under my breath, as the images I'd seen on the news the night before, the ones of folks being swept away by floodwater currents bearing a striking resemblance to the scene before us, flashed in my mind. *I'm going to be so pissed if this is how we die.*

Suddenly out of nowhere, three young men miraculously appeared, chugging an old boat down the street. They were draped in camouflage rain ponchos.

"Are you guys looking to cross?" they yelled over the sound of the boat.

"Yes!" we shouted back. "Can you take us?"

"Most of the way," they said. "We can get you to the bridge. You might have to wade a bit after you cross."

We clambered into the boat: Marcus, me, and poor, shivering Soca. As the boat chugged down the street, we passed houses flooded to their rooflines. Clearly, there was no way we would have been able to get through on foot.

The men ferried us about a mile to the bridge, where the water was only as high as our ankles. We got out. "It shouldn't be too deep on the other side," smiled one of the young men. "Good luck!" Gratitude washed over us: it was painful to imagine what would have happened if we had attempted to cross on our own.

We offered them money. "Take it!" Marcus insisted, over the sound of the wind and the boat's motor, as he tried to push the soggy bills into their hands. "For beer!"

"No, no, no . . ." They shook their heads emphatically, but I protested: "Seriously, you guys are angels; you've officially earned your place in heaven. You don't have to be good anymore! Take the money. Blow it all in one place. Live a little!"

The men laughed but flat-out refused. They just turned their little boat around, waving as they left. We watched as they disappeared, and then we continued across the bridge. On the other side, we waded the remaining half-mile through torrential rain and chest-deep water to Dustin, who was waiting worriedly in his pick-up truck. Relieved to see each other, we climbed in and Dustin whisked us to his home. Our shoulders finally relaxed when Marcus and I at last laid eyes on our daughter, wrapping her in a soggy hug. Dustin's wife, Cheryl, greeted us with towels, hot tea, and bowls of steaming soup. For several days, their family kept ours warm, dry, and fed while we regrouped.

These were only the first of many kindnesses we received in the weeks following the flood. Friends from around the country had been following what was happening to Houston on the news, and they rallied together. Within days, cleaning supplies and clothing and small appliances and even guitar picks for our musician-daughter were flooding my post office box. Dozens of total strangers showed up to our home to help us clean out ruined belongings and demolish our filthy walls, which were already showing signs of mold.

One day a guy we'd never seen before appeared at our front door. He'd driven all the way from New Orleans that morning, and he asked what he could do to help. "You Houstonians were so good to us during Hurricane Katrina," he said. "Driving in was the least I could do. Should I grab my tools?" He was already making his way to the bed of his pickup truck before I could answer. He spent the day helping us remove drywall and transferring our fetid clothing and furniture to the curb to be taken away. Then, since all the hotels in town were filled with displaced Houstonians, he just got in his car and drove the five hours back to New Orleans that night.

I never even got his name.

Years later, as I look back at the days during and following the flood, I still get choked up thinking about how much beauty and kindness surrounded my family and me. But what's odd is that although we lost everything—and I mean, *everything*—my memories of the devastation are fuzzy. What stands out in sharp relief is the unbridled generosity that was offered to us at every turn. The strangers who appeared out of nowhere, the friends who organized shopping lists to get basic necessities to us: their activism literally saved us when our lives had been upended in the most staggering way. Throughout those dark days, what stays with me the most are the moments of light these people provided. These memories overwhelm me with gratitude. And yes, weirdly, remembering that kindness inspires a kind of joy.

While my family and I were the beneficiaries of the activism of these kind folks, I suspect that they, too, experienced something akin to joy simply from doing their generous work. Take my friend Aimee Woodall, for example. Her home was mercifully spared the effects of Harvey, but as soon as the storm passed, she and another friend were overcome with the urge to do something to help their devastated community. Together, these two entrepreneurs found some office space and launched a distribution center they called the Giving Hub. News of their efforts spread quickly, and over the following three weeks, Aimee and her friend marshalled the efforts of more than four hundred volunteers, some from as far away as Canada, and moved more than one hundred thousand items like food, water, diapers, and other critical goods to families in flood-ravaged locations throughout Texas. It was such a heroic undertaking that the Giving Hub garnered the attention of the Obama Foundation, which celebrated them at its inaugural summit the following autumn.

When Aimee speaks of the experience now, she doesn't mention the havoc and desperation that she witnessed during those weeks in 2017. She doesn't even talk about what it felt like to be invited to the Obama Foundation summit. Instead, she remembers being a part of something big, and beautiful, and generous.

"What I witnessed during the storm is something I wish we could see in each other all the time," remembers Aimee. "Just people jumping in to solve problems together, without needing a storm as a catalyst." Aimee's emotions around that time included both awe at the work of more than four hundred selfless volunteers, as well as wonder at the fact that together they could serve families during their most desperate hours. Her memories of the Giving Hub experience fill her with meaning and hope and faith. And the combination of those emotions? Well, it feels a lot like joy.

This phenomenon—the emergence of joy from pain and difficulty—is noted in the incredible book *The Book of Joy*, by His Holiness the Dalai Lama and Archbishop Desmond Tutu. This work was the result of the two religious leaders meeting in Dharamsala, India, to celebrate the Dalai Lama's eightieth birthday. While there, they collaborated with writer Douglas Abrams to record their thoughts on the true meaning of joy. Although these two men both hold venerable positions, they have also endured profound challenges. Following the brutal suppression of the Tibetan national uprising in Lhasa by Chinese troops in 1959, the Dalai Lama was forced to escape, at the age of only twenty-three. His journey to India took three weeks on foot, and he has been living in Dharamsala, in exile from his home, ever since. Archbishop Tutu grew up in South Africa under apartheid, the institutionalized racist regime that reigned in the country from 1948 until the early 1990s. His journey from childhood to priesthood was difficult, made even more complicated by an eighteen-month bout of tuberculosis that brought him near death. Later, when the apartheid government arrested and imprisoned many political leaders, including Nelson Mandela, Archbishop Tutu often acted as the de facto leader of the anti-apartheid movement, until the regime finally fell in 1994. At the time of his meeting with the Dalai Lama in 2015 to record their thoughts for their joint book, Archbishop Tutu was suffering from prostate cancer and had been for decades.

So these two holy men are no strangers to struggle and sadness. Yet it is obvious that they are men of incredible joy. Throughout the book, Abrams remarks on their constant laughing and sharing gestures of genuine affection. And early on, during the first part of their weeklong visit, Archbishop Tutu shared a few thoughts about joy.

"It's wonderful to discover that what we want is not actually happiness," he began. "It is not actually what I would speak of. I would speak of joy. Joy subsumes happiness. Joy is the far greater thing. Think of a mother who is going to give birth. Almost all of us want to escape pain. And mothers know that they are going to have pain, the great pain of giving birth. But they accept it. And even after the most painful labor, once the baby is out, you can't measure the mother's joy. It is one of those incredible things that joy can come so quickly from suffering."

Archbishop Tutu is right: this *is* a wonderful discovery. Even during times of great challenge, joy often sits alongside suffering. Mere happiness, though? Not so much. And when it comes to activism, this distinction between joy and happiness is an important one to make. This fact—that joy is more profound than happiness—opens up the possibility that we can find joy when our work as activists requires us to witness—and experience—hardship.

But can joy actually be *cultivated?* Is it possible that by focusing our efforts on this joy, we might even be able to change our outlook to be more optimistic about the outcomes of our activism work? Better still, could joy even *fuel* our activism?

Not only do I answer yes to these questions; there's also a relatively new science around why this might be the case.

♦ ♦ ♦

Several years ago a friend of mine went through a messy breakup which had left her devastated. As she was speaking with her therapist, she let her outlook spiral downward. What if I'm flawed? she wondered. What if I don't deserve affection or true connection? Exhausted, she finally voiced her deepest fear: perhaps she would never, ever be truly loved again.

She waited for the therapist's response, but the therapist simply smiled gently. "You understand, of course," said the therapist, "that you have evidence to suggest otherwise."

This answer might be my favorite thing ever. The phrase "You have evidence to suggest otherwise" is *way* more powerful than the more common "This too shall pass." There's an additional subtext to it, an unspoken sentiment that indicates "you know this to be true." You have evidence to suggest otherwise: it's a gentle admonition to get out of your head and get into the facts. To be clear, this isn't unchecked Pollyanna-esque smile-the-pain-away talk. If you think about it, we've all had moments of beauty in our lives, and there's nothing to suggest similar moments won't occur again. But as my friend's therapist indicated, once we've allowed and acknowledged our pain, it's possible to gently shift our outlook toward a more positive mindset by using a concrete, evidence-based way to access joy.

This shift perfectly illustrates the fundamental power of positive psychology. Described as the scientific study of human potential and positive aspects of the human experience that make life worth living, positive psychology is a relatively new field. When Dr. Martin Seligman assumed his position as president of the American Psychological Association in 1998, there was a seventeen-to-one bias in psychology: for every study conducted about happiness, there were seventeen studies of depression and disease. Dr. Seligman found this bias myopic: if science paid such close attention to mental illness while ignoring what makes people mentally healthy, what faulty assumptions emerged?

So Seligman devoted his life to expanding the focus of modern psychology and is now considered the father of positive psychology. Rather than fixating on pathologies and mental illnesses, Seligman posits that it also makes sense to study the positive attributes and practices that allow us to achieve our potential. At the individual level, this means considering positive emotions such as "well-being, contentment, and satisfaction (in the past); hope and optimism (for the future); and flow and happiness (in the present)." This may seem intuitive to us now, but when Seligman chose positive psychology as the theme of his work in 1998, these concepts were revolutionary.

Since that time, the field has grown exponentially. I first learned of it when I stumbled upon the wildly popular TED talk titled "The Happy Secret to Better Work," given by author, psychologist, and thought leader Shawn Achor. In a riveting and very funny twelve minutes, Achor effectively argues that we can actually *train our brains* to be more joyful. His research indicates that when our brains are positive, they perform significantly better than when our brains are negative, neutral, or stressed. "Your intelligence rises, your creativity rises, your energy levels rise," he enthuses. "In fact, we've found that very single business outcome improves."

These are incredibly bold words. I was so intrigued by Achor's declarations that I immediately sought training with the Wholebeing Institute, which bases its program on positive psychology, to supplement my leadership coaching practice. And in my experience, Achor's assertions appear valid. I've witnessed my own clients' lives be transformed: when they begin to see their experiences, skills, and gifts in a more positive light, and access concrete evidence of their own past successes, they become far more hopeful about their futures and more energized to achieve their goals. As a result, they become more confident about their own abilities and they face challenges with more optimism. In essence, they become more *joyful*. This is true whether those goals are related to their careers or causes about which they have a great passion. By cultivating their own joy—literally, *practicing* joy—they fuel their own motivation and make huge strides toward achieving their goals, activism-related or otherwise.

Often, when my clients cultivate these practices of joy, they make *meaning* as a consequence: they find ways to be of significance, relevance, or value. This isn't surprising: unlike happiness, joy frequently includes *meaning*, as evidenced in the stories of my superhero friend Aimee of the Giving Hub, of home healthcare workers Sam and Grace, and of Archbishop Tutu. The concept of joy based in meaning is nowhere better expressed than in the book *Man's Search for Meaning* by Viktor Frankl. Frankl, an Austrian psychologist and a Holocaust survivor, offered his services as a therapist to fellow prisoners at the Auschwitz concentration camp. After he was released, inspired by what he witnessed and learned from his comrades during his imprisonment, he wrote his seminal work in nine days. Frankl had realized, most profoundly, that the true purpose of life is rooted in the quest for meaning. In his words, "There is nothing in the world, I venture to say, that would so effectively help one to survive even the worst conditions as the knowledge that there is a meaning in one's life." He continues, "Life ultimately means taking the responsibility to find the right answer to its problems and to fulfill the tasks which it constantly sets for each individual."

Sounds an awful lot like activism, doesn't it?

According to Frankl, meaning comes primarily from three sources: doing something significant, caring for others, and summoning courage during difficult times. Even more interesting, he believes that when we pursue and practice a meaningful life, joy necessarily follows. In fact, he insists, "it only does so as the unintended side-effect of one's dedication to a cause greater than oneself."

This, of course, has huge implications for the work we do as activists and for how we live our lives. If we try to find happiness solely for ourselves, we may miss it entirely. But if we work for the causes around which we have passion—especially if we do it in a spirit of caring, courage, and generosity—joy may naturally follow. The trick, of course, is ensuring that we practice our activism in a truly intentional, mindful way. By doing so, what we experience may even feel transcendent.

◆ ◆ ◆

Since joy and meaning are intertwined, I began to wonder whether faith and spirituality are related as well. After all, Frankl and his patients were Jewish; was it possible that faith or spirituality played a part in their cultivation of meaning and therefore joy? More specifically, since meaning is a necessary component of joy, must activists always nurture a faith practice as well?

In an attempt to find the answer to this question, whenever I spoke to the activists and lightmakers I interviewed for this book, I asked how faith or spirituality informs their advocacy work, if at all. To be honest, I suspected that everyone I interviewed would profess at least some belief in a higher power.

I was wrong. Their answers varied widely. A few responded that their religious faith traditions and beliefs are interwoven into every aspect of their work. Others practice a faith but don't really think about the teachings of their faith as they advocate. Still others don't have a faith tradition at all, and a few describe themselves as atheists.

This surprised me—especially since almost without exception, they all referred to their motivation for doing their work as an impulse that came from something bigger than themselves. Only after a few interviews—including conversations with my friends Aaron Billard and Sean Fitzpatrick—did I begin to piece together what I was witnessing.

Aaron Billard is the creative mind behind Unvirtuous Abbey, a Twitter account run by "digital monks praying for people with first world problems." I first started following the account about ten years ago, when its author was anonymous. I loved its irreverent but lighthearted way of poking fun at some of the more strident aspects of Christianity, often using pop culture references, but always without being mean-spirited. Over time, however, I began to realize that the Unvirtuous Abbey account is only superficially about making people laugh; it's also a reminder that we are all interconnected and deserving of love and belonging. Over the years, the "monks" began to make more and more pointed barbs against racism, sexism, and other forms of discrimination, as well as more global declarations of how much we all need each other. This message of inclusivity is deeply attractive: hundreds of thousands of people all around the world follow Unvirtuous Abbey.

It was apparent pretty early on that the "digital abbot"—as the person writing the Unvirtuous Abbey tweets called himself—practiced a faith. I began to wonder if he was actually a member of the clergy. Years later, I learned that he is: Aaron is a minister with the United Church of Canada. So when I began writing this book, I knew I wanted to ask him about how he uses both his humor and his faith in his digital activism.

In addition to being funny, Aaron is exactly as you'd hope any minister would be: gentle and kind and thoughtful. We'd sent messages to each other over the years but had never actually met, and yet seeing him on my screen during our videoconferencing call felt like reuniting with an old friend.

I began with my standard interview questions: I asked him where the idea for Unvirtuous Abbey had come from, and how it had evolved over the years. Eventually we got around to my question about how his faith may or may not inform his activism. Aaron paused for a good moment before answering. "Well," he said slowly, "when you dabble in the spiritual arts, you have to be careful."

Dabble in the spiritual arts? Well, *there's* a phrase I didn't expect. "Say more," I urged. "Is it possible for, say, someone who is atheist or agnostic to 'dabble in the spiritual arts'? Is activism, by definition, spiritual?"

"Oh, for sure," was his immediate response:

Activism is definitely spiritual. What I love about activism is that it takes me out of myself to work for the peace of the community around me. As a minister I try to do this as a follower of Jesus, who teaches me to feed his sheep, not convert or shame them. And Unvirtuous Abbey is part of that activism and spiritual practice. For someone else who is a member of another faith tradition—or none at all—their activism practice might involve something entirely different. Maybe they work with addicts. Or maybe they create access to clean needles and a safe space to drop off dirty needles. It all plugs in together—doing what we can, where we can.

Weeks later I had a conversation with Sean Fitzpatrick, who echoed the idea that activism can be spiritual. Sean is the executive director of The Jung Center of Houston, a nonprofit dedicated to "providing pathways to find a deeper meaning in everyday life." Even though he was raised Catholic, Sean tells me he has "a complicated relationship with Christianity and Catholicism" and that he does not currently practice a faith; even so, he holds master's degrees in religious studies and clinical psychology and a doctorate in psychology. We had met through the Houston Coalition Against Hate, an organization in which we are both active members, and I liked him immediately. Given Sean's thoughtful nature, I knew that if I asked him about activism and spirituality, he'd have an interesting perspective. Happily, he agreed to let me interview him.

When we met, I dove right in. "I'm trying to figure out whether spirituality is required to cultivate joy and also to make activism sustainable," I said. "And you have degrees in this stuff. How would you define 'spirituality'?"

He smiled, inhaled deeply, and thought for a moment. "I mean . . ." He paused again. "It's about experience, and it's about experiences of meaning."

That word again, I thought. "Experiences of *meaning*?" I repeated. "Yeah." He nodded slowly and said,

I think that's the beginning point. If we draw it more broadly than that, we start to get into language that might sound poetic, but also language that starts to rely on ideas of divinity that don't translate across all cultures. I think the emphasis here is on the word *experience*. In fact, I had a professor when I was a student at the University of Houston, an Episcopal priest named Pittman McGehee, who once shared something that I think is relevant. He used to be dean of Christchurch Cathedral here in Houston, but he left active ministry to become a Jungian analyst. I remember he once said to me that spirituality—or spiritual experience—is accidental, and spiritual practice makes you accident-prone.

It was my turn to laugh. Sean smiled. "For that reason, I do believe practicing activism is about being in experiences in which you are connected with others and connected in an immediate way to living your values," he said. "There are elements of those experiences which, even though maybe we wouldn't immediately think of the words *mystical* or *spiritual* to describe them, are definitely spiritual in nature."

There it is: activism, when approached with an intentional mindset, is all about creating experiences of meaning. Activism means taking responsibility to find answers to the world's problems, dedicating yourself to a cause greater than your own interests. Activism doesn't require a faith home or a spiritual practice; yet activism can feel very spiritual in nature.

The lightmakers and activist friends I interviewed for this book expressed what it feels like to answer a deeply held, personal call to make the world better. They described the ways in which answering that call feels transcendent, irrespective of any religious or faith tradition. Activism, rooted in meaning, helps to fulfill the activist's purpose.

And in the words of Frankl: joy necessarily follows.

3 | ON BANGS, WHISPERS, AND TRINIDADIAN RUM

"I'm not saying you're stupid, but you're certainly acting that way."

He stood over me, his face flushed and breath growing ragged. He was glowering, and even the white hair in his eyebrows seemed to be standing on end. My coworker's jawline contracted as he stared at me, holding my gaze, and he searched my face to see if his words had hit their mark.

Still seated at my desk, I took a deep breath. I hadn't realized that we'd raised our voices, but judging from the way the world had fallen silent outside of my office door, it was clear we had. This was a first. While it wasn't unusual for account managers to be frustrated with the limits we lawyers put on their deals, they usually understood where we were coming from. We all recognized these deal limits were part of the challenging relationship between sales and legal. After all, we were just trying to keep the company out of trouble—and them out of jail. While the account managers might protest, in the end, they all knew that the legal team had the company's best interests at heart.

All, that is, except for this guy, still looming over me, still awaiting my response.

Without breaking eye contact, I took another deep breath. "You may be right," I began, carefully modulating my voice. "I might be stupid. But even if that's true, it's the law. You might have broken it, and I'm not backing down."

He flipped out. For the next few minutes, he railed on and on, claiming that I had no idea "how business is done." I was clearly rooting for him to fail, he yelled, and he threatened to have my job. Finally, he stormed out of my office, muttering obscenities over his shoulder as he left.

I sat, stunned, trying to collect myself. No one had ever yelled at me at work before, and for a second, I didn't know what to do. I checked the clock: it was three-thirty. Forget it: I was done for the day. I closed my laptop, threw it into my work bag, and walked out of my office door.

In the hallway, my coworker Michelle met me wide-eyed, having overheard the ruckus from my office. "Are you alright?" she half-whispered, her voice heavy with concern.

"Yes," I answered weakly. "But I'm going home now."

She nodded, stepping aside to let me pass. "Take it easy, okay?"

I offered her a wan smile as I walked by. I don't remember how I made it to my car or drove the ten minutes home, but when I arrived, Marcus was there to greet me. As soon as he saw the expression on my face, his eyes widened. "What the hell happened to you?"

That was all the opening I needed. "You will not *believe* this," I said, launching into a rant of my own. The more I described my coworker's inappropriate behavior, the more alarmed Marcus became. Finally, thirty minutes in, he offered softly, "Maybe your dad would have some advice?"

My father had spent his career as an energy industry executive. Beginning as an entry-level petroleum engineer—and the first Black professional in his multinational employer's American offices—he retired as a vice president of a Fortune 500 oil company. I often look to my father as a mentor, but especially in handling work-related issues. I picked up the phone.

"Ka-REN!" Dad exclaimed, in his lilting Trinidadian accent. "What can I do for you today?"

Unfortunately for my father, I hadn't quite calmed down yet, so without much preface, I told him everything: how I'd asked this coworker for an explanation for his actions, how he didn't *exactly* call me stupid but claimed that I was "acting that way." I told him how this guy threatened to have my job—despite my reminder that my job was to ensure that our company acted within the law. Dad listened attentively, only interrupting a few times to ask some clarifying questions.

Finally he spoke.

"You're right to be angry," he said slowly. "He was out of line. Where's Marcus? Is Marcus at home?"

"Yes . . . ?" I responded, confused.

"Put him on."

I handed Marcus the phone. "Hello?" Then: "Yes sir—" he listened, furrowing his brow. "Okay . . . okay. Okay, I will. Here she is."

Marcus handed me the phone. "Your dad said I need to give you rum," he said, walking toward the liquor cabinet.

I smiled. "Thanks, Dad," I said, finally calming down.

Dad gave me a few more bits of advice, telling me that I needed to breathe through my anger and take the rest of the day to relax. "You can think about next moves after a good night's sleep," he reassured me. "Once you're rested, I have no doubt you'll find a creative solution." By the time we hung up, my husband had returned with a shockingly large pour of Trinidadian rum.

About thirty minutes later, halfway through my rum and feeling a bit lightheaded, I thought of my dad's words. It dawned on me:

maybe it *was* time for a change. Notwithstanding the day's events, I actually had a great job: I was a lawyer in technology, which was exactly the kind of law I enjoyed practicing. I enjoyed my bosses, and they seemed to value my contribution. But the entire reason for in-house counsel is to ensure everyone follows the law, and that purpose, in and of itself, is bound to be fraught with conflict. If the only way I could deal with resistance to my advice was to rage—requiring my father and husband to collude to get me drunk—then maybe I wasn't cut out for the profession after all. The truth was that software licensing and corporate law, while interesting, didn't fill me with *purpose*. And working in the energy industry was becoming problematic for me: I had learned about the adverse impact that oil and gas exploration and production, which my employer enabled, had on the environment. I was concerned by my own role in harming the earth. So when I had a bad day, I certainly didn't believe in my work enough to make a hard day worth the stress.

I put my half-drunk glass of rum in the sink, took a shower, and tried not to think about my job for the rest of the evening. The next morning, before heading into work, I found an old journal I'd purchased years ago. I cracked the spine and turned to the first blank page. With my pen, I scrawled at the top of the page:

If I didn't practice law, what would I do?
How could this provide meaning and purpose to my life?
How could I make the world better?

I sat for a minute, waiting for the answers to come. And then I began writing.

There's so much wrong with the world that making a list of every way you could try to make it better—every cause you could care about—would take a lot more space than one journal offers. Even if you managed to narrow which issues are most important to you, you'd be faced with more decisions: What do you do to help? Do you march? Write your government representative? Run for office? Raise money? Give money? Protest? Then, what about the remaining causes? Would focusing on one issue mean you no longer cared about the others? And really, what sort of impact could you—a single person—make to fight these ills in the first place? How could you get any joy out of working in advocacy when anything you do barely makes a dent?

How would you even begin?

I asked this question of several activist friends, and overwhelmingly, one bit of advice kept coming up: you get curious about the call.

Take my friend Jess Weiner. I've known Jess for many years and have even worked with her on a few projects. She has an easy laugh and a joyful, confident spirit, with a fierce determination to change the world. Ever since she was a student at Penn State University in the 1990s, Jess has worked tirelessly to support the rights of women and girls. Nowadays, even if you don't know her name, you likely know her work. Her consulting services are, in large part, the reason the Dove brand launched its Campaign for Real Beauty in 2004, resulting in advertising, workshops, talk shows, and a global conversation around the message that physical appearance should be a source of confidence rather than anxiety. Jess was also a key member of the team behind Mattel's decision to offer Barbie dolls with more diverse body sizes and their launch of a more gender-inclusive doll line. Disney has relied on her guidance as they've brought the princesses of their feature films into an era of empowerment. Fast Company even named her an "advo-consultant": her entire business is activism and advocacy, helping brands elevate communication around how women and girls are seen and portrayed in the media, and therefore becoming champions themselves in gender justice.

But that's not all. In addition to her professional life, she and her husband advise a girls' school in Guatemala, and she serves on the board of She Should Run, a nonpartisan nonprofit that works to increase the number of women running for office. Because Jess has been so successful in her advocacy of women and girls, I knew she would be a fount of information for those looking to enter into activism.

As I prepared for our time together, I realized that even though I'd known Jess for years, I had no idea how she'd been called to activism. So I began our videoconference one midsummer day by asking how she got started in gender justice work and what advice she would give to someone who didn't know how to begin.

Jess's awakening to activism was intense, to say the least. "What calls you to enter into activism can be a whisper, or it can be a bang," she began. "In my case, I was walking back from studying at the library at Penn State, and I got caught in the mob."

Jess was referring to a tradition at Penn State called the Mifflin Streak: during the week before finals, residents of one of the dormitory halls run through campus stark naked. It sounds like relatively lighthearted fun; however, when Jess was a student the event often devolved into something far darker. The small crowd of a few dozen streakers turned into a mob of thousands of men who yelled obscenities at women students, and worse. "I had never been inappropriately groped or touched prior to that in my life. But that night, I had four or five different people's hands on me as I was trying to get back to my dorm room. It was the first time I could recall being deeply, deeply terrified."

"Holy crap, Jess," I gasped. "I'm so, so sorry."

She smiled dryly, but kept going. "What tipped the scales for me, though, and really activated me, was when I got back to my residence hall, they'd locked the door and I couldn't get in."

My eyes grew wide. "Wait, what?"

"Right." Her smile was now tinged with anger. "So I started banging on the door, and finally the resident advisor appeared. When she saw me, she opened the door and began scolding me for being out."

Jess frowned at the memory, but continued. "Now remember, I was a freshman, so I immediately felt like I broke the rules and that it was my fault that this had happened to me. But I later found out that the university had actually asked the resident assistants to lock the women in the residence halls that night."

My jaw dropped. "I . . ."

"Yeah. Let me repeat this: the resident assistants were told to lock the doors and keep us inside, while the men ran amok on campus."

Jess continued,

That, for me, was a turning point: an awakening. I decided to say something about it to the administration, but they did nothing. In the aftermath, as the university continued to not take me seriously, it really dawned on me that this wasn't okay. I tried to figure out what the root of my anger was, and I realized that yes, of course these guys were behaving in a criminal manner, and that was infuriating; but ultimately, the crux of my fury was that the university was condoning it. I was, in essence, giving money to a system that was condoning the interference of my education in favor of the criminal behavior of the men on campus. *That wasn't okay.* It was an awakening experience that was hard to ignore. And it opened my eyes to begin to look for oppression in all corners of that campus.

"I imagine it did!" I said.

"So to your question: what called *me* to be an activist was a bang. But for some people, there isn't a single awakening experience. Instead, it's just a whisper. And I've talked to young people who hear the whisper, and they want to get involved more, but they don't quite know how. When they ask for my advice, I always tell them to keep listening to the whisper. Don't ignore it. Keep listening, and let it guide you to do the very first thing, even if it's just getting curious."

It's not surprising that Jess's horrifying experience catapulted her into a life of advocacy. But interestingly, the idea that a call to activism might come in the form of a whisper was common. Several other lightmakers described it in exactly the same way, and often, they shared that becoming still and paying attention to the whisper of intuition was crucial in their journey to determine which causes to take up and fight for. My friend Brad Montague is a great example. He found that paying attention to that whisper, even as he experimented with different types of activism, finally led to his true calling.

Brad is a filmmaker and an author, and if you ask him why he does what he does, he'll tell you it's because children need to know that their voices matter. And he's had the heart of an activist for his entire life: as a child, he was so moved by the commercials that often came on during children's television programming that his parents once had to talk him down from destroying all the matches in their home just so he could do his part in preventing forest fires.

I first became aware of Brad's work when I stumbled across a little film he had created and shared online that stars his young brother-in-law, Robby. In the video, Robby, also known as Kid President, dances and plays with a football on a deserted football field during the golden hour, while earnestly giving a pep talk that reminds viewers that "we were made to be awesome." In his dark little business suit and presidential red tie, Robby is sweet and sincere, and his pep talk—which draws wisdom from poet Robert Frost to Michael Jordan's role in the movie *Space Jam*—is an undeniably emphatic call for us all, no matter our age or background, to be our better selves.

Brad describes the process of creating the video in his book *Becoming Better Grownups*. He first shared Robby's pep talk video online on a Thursday evening, and by Sunday, it had already been viewed a million times. Not quite a decade later, as I write these words, it has been viewed more than 46 million times.

Apparently the world still needs pep talks!

In person, Brad exudes the same warmth, sweetness, and sincerity as his kid brother-in-law does. He tuned in for our videoconference from Montague Workshop headquarters in Tennessee, and it was clear that his workspace is designed to encourage all the joy and whimsy so apparent in his work. I was thrilled to listen to Brad's thoughts about activism. Unlike Jess's call—the bang that came from an intense and traumatic experience in college—he experienced the call to change the world as a quiet one.

"I feel like we listen too much to the loudest things, sometimes," he began slowly, thoughtfully. "But I believe that the moment we allow ourselves to hear that whisper is the beginning of unlocking our true adventure, the real thing that we're here to do. The more we pay attention to that, the more we begin to add beauty to the world."

I smiled. "You're the second person I've spoken to who describes it as a whisper," I said. "What does that mean to you, exactly?"

He thought for a moment. "Well, I see it almost as tuning to a specific frequency, like a radio," he explained. "You tune in to hear it, and you have to really listen and hear the need and what's calling you to help. But you also have to have the humility to acknowledge that you don't have all the answers. I think sometimes acknowledging the pain is the first step."

He paused. "In my case, I had deep beliefs that things needed to change," he continued, "and in college and shortly after college, I certainly participated in marches and protests that would traditionally fall under the heading 'activism.' But over time, as I worked with young people, I became inspired by what *they* were doing to change the world. I realized that they weren't just trying to copy the adults."

"What were they doing?" I was intrigued.

"Well, what they *weren't* doing was just making signs and banners with statements on them. Instead, they were activists in the purest sense: they saw a need, their hearts were broken, and because their hearts were already open, they thought to themselves, 'We've got to do something about this.'"

His smile grew soft. "I became more and more aware that what I really wanted to do—what the whisper was telling me—was to help and enable the communication of these kids *with each other*. I wanted to help them speak their ideas and help them continue to do so in a healthy way. I saw my place in advocacy as becoming one of showing kids how to keep being activists—and how to keep doing so *joyfully*."

My own call to activism was definitely a whisper. I knew I wanted to do something meaningful and purposeful with my life, and I knew that I needed to do something that would serve the world. The problem was that I wasn't sure what to do or how to do it. I was overwhelmed by all those questions about what advocacy could look like, and I didn't even know what to advocate *for*. I needed to slow down the questions I was asking and really consider them. I had to figure out what I loved to do. Determine which causes were important to me. Discover if I had any skills that could be harnessed in service of those causes. And it was out of that desperation for quiet consideration that years ago, after that run-in with my coworker, I decided to grab a journal.

Confession: growing up, I thought keeping a journal was terminally childish and hopelessly self-indulgent. I held this opinion firmly, despite never having actually known anyone who kept a journal. My father, while always intrigued by story and legacy, was always far too busy in his job to keep a journal. And I suspect that my mother, at least at that time, would have thought diaries frivolous and vain. Even if I had seriously considered journaling, that one episode of the TV show *The Brady Bunch*—the one featuring the histrionics of a young Marcia Brady when she learns her journal has been inadvertently donated to charity—well, that alone would have been enough to convince me never to begin one in the first place.

By the time I reached adulthood, I'd stopped thinking of journaling as childish and instead viewed journaling as something only creative people did. I was decidedly uncreative—or so I thought. I came by that belief honestly, by the way: when I was in my twenties, my father called me into his home office. "Here are all the files from your childhood," he said. "You're grown now—you can take them."

In his file cabinet was every single document that recorded my life: invoices for dance lessons, medical bills, random bits of art, and all the report cards I'd received from preschool through university. As I went through the documents, one report card in particular stood out. It was a yellowed piece of paper signed by my elementary school teacher. My eyes fell on the following words: "Karen excels at English and Math but does not show any artistic ability." *Ouch.*

For the record, I never knew about this report card until my father gave me those files. Yet it explains why, for my entire life, I was gently steered away from any artistic pursuits whatsoever. "I think I want to be an architect," I'd say to my parents. "That's nice, dear, but you're more of a math person," they'd counter; "Have you considered structural engineering?" It worked: I ended up going to university and earning a bachelor's degree in civil engineering. It wasn't until much later, when I was about to graduate from law school, that I even dared consider pursuing anything artistic—which I did by buying that old camera. But creating something that came directly from imagination, and not as a result of legal research or a cursory understanding of light physics? *Artists* do that. I certainly was no artist.

So my decision to crack open a journal the morning after my clash with that colleague felt decidedly out of character. But desperate times call for desperate measures. I grabbed a journal that early morning because I didn't know *what* to think.

My sudden desire to become a diarist wasn't completely devoid of logic. I was on the verge of blowing up an eighteen-year law career with no plan for my future. Putting something on paper seemed like the rational first step. I had a sneaking suspicion that by writing down the swirling thoughts in my head and seeing them in black-and-white, I could make sense of them all. Writing in that journal wasn't about expressing myself or about creating art. My journal was about finding some semblance of clarity. About searching for a clue. My journal was a *tool*.

I began writing every morning before work. Over the next few months, as I prepared an exit strategy from my job, a clearer picture began to emerge—if not of what my next move would be, then at least what it *wouldn't* be. I developed a more detailed image of what was important to me and what I wanted my work and life to stand for. By the time I left my employment a few months later, I had become clear about what my beliefs were and what issues mattered most to me. I had even discovered what my gifts and talents were, if not the exact way I was going to use them to change the world. I had become more rooted in my own values.

It turns out I was onto something with this journaling practice. While conventional thinking paints journaling as solely a form of self-expression, engineers, scientists, artists, and creatives of all backgrounds use their journals for far more: everything from capturing progress made toward goals, results of successful and failed experiments, detailed logs of story ideas, and even painting techniques. Julia Cameron, author of *The Artist's Way*, which has become the creative bible for artistic folks, has a devoted journaling practice that she calls "morning pages": three handwritten pages of anything that's on her mind, without any regard for spelling, grammar, or even creativity. She maintains that morning pages allow us to "clarify our yearnings. They keep an eye on our goals. They may provoke us, coax us, comfort us, even cajole us, as well as prioritize and synchronize the day at hand. If we are drifting, the pages will point that out. They will point the way True North."

Even former US president Barack Obama has found the practice of journaling essential to his work. In 2012, in his interview as *Time* magazine's Person of the Year, he revealed that, in the days after the election, he began "scribbling his hopes on a yellow legal pad." He explained, "In my life, writing has been an important exercise to clarify what I believe, what I I see, what I care about, what my deepest values are. The process of converting a jumble of thoughts into coherent sentences makes you ask tougher questions." Now, Obama was dealing with issues that could mean life or death for the citizens of his country (and the world, for that matter), and Cameron's book, *The Artist's Way*, was initially intended for people in artistic professions. But what is the process of charting our course to change the world—fraught with profound implications for ourselves and the people around us—if not an exercise in innovation? What is the process of identifying our gifts and talents—and how we can use them to serve the world—if not a call to tap into our most creative selves?

Years later, I remain an avid journaler. Along my activism path, even as I began to understand where my destination was, my decisions have shifted and evolved. Forks and crossroads along the journey have become worth a detour or two. Writing my thoughts in a journal allows me to tap into a wisdom that, while accessible when I'm giving advice to other people, requires a bit of digging in order to access for myself.

The luminescent Valarie Kaur agrees with me. My friend Valarie is a Sikh American activist, filmmaker, faith leader, and author of *See No Stranger*. In her work, Valarie often faces painful stories of violence arising from racial and religious discrimination, as well as misogyny and sexual and gender bigotry; her advocacy philosophy of revolutionary love in meeting these challenges has placed her "at the forefront of progressive change," according to the Center for American Progress. Revolutionary love is inspired, in many ways, by her own maternal experience. In her Sikh Prayer for America, delivered to a congregation at Metropolitan African Methodist Episcopal Church in Washington, DC on New Year's Eve in 2016, she called on us all to heed the wisdom of the midwife: to ensure that we breathe—rest, restore, and regroup—before each push toward social change.

When we sat down to talk, Valarie shared that she often turns to her journal as a form of self-guidance and self-care. "I've found that all of us have a different role to play at any given moment, and our breathing and pushing looks different too, depending on who we are, and what our activism in the moment looks like," she explained. "Whenever I wondered, 'What should my role be in this moment?' I came to hear the voice of a very wise woman inside me. Audre Lorde says we can learn how to mother ourselves, and I'm finally learning how to mother myself. I have to get quiet, because the voice is quiet."

There's that whisper again. She continued,

And truly, my practice in learning how to love myself is getting my chatter and the voice of the little critic in my mind quiet enough to hear what the wise woman has to tell me. So, Karen, I literally have a journal that I keep close, and I call it my Wise Woman journal. Three times a day, I write in it as my own wise woman, and she begins by telling me the state of my body. *You are tired today . . . this is where the energy is.* . . . Then, while listening, I reflect in the pages the thing that I am most called to do. Once I put the journal away, I do that.

"This is incredible," I responded, my eyes wide. "I love this, Valarie: this idea of a constant companion for a quick, periodic check-in every day."

She grinned. "Yes, but I'll also summon her for the big, big life decisions. Listening and paying attention to the voice of the wise woman inside of me is how I discern my role. It's a disciplined practice."

Cultivating a disciplined practice of listening to your own inner wisdom is instrumental in ensuring your path is the right one for you to follow. That's true whether you're just beginning your advocacy journey, as I was, or whether you're a seasoned activist, as Valarie is. In all cases, however, a journal is a perfect way to slow down and listen to your quiet voice. You can begin by simply asking yourself questions, as I did. Write the questions at the top of your page. Pause for a moment to see what answers arise, and then write them down.

In the alternative, you can use the exercise Brad Montague offers to young people to help them with their own discernment:

When we talk about this to young people, there's this—not a formula, exactly, but a way of asking a bunch of "wonder" questions. For example, the first question I might ask them to consider is, "I wonder who needs help?" That list might be long, but it will start the juices flowing. Then usually, I prompt them to ask themselves, "I wonder what they need most right now?" and encourage them to brainstorm that list. The next question I prompt them to think about is, "I wonder who might work with me to help them get that or have that?" Once they've made a list of potential helpers, I finally ask them to consider, "I wonder what the most wonderful thing could be that we all do together?" This process leads to more and more and more wonder.

Brad's discernment process, which leads with wonder, allows for the imagination to make so many connections and so much light. "And it's a great guide for kids because it allows them to see that they're not in it alone, and it's not this big problem that they have to figure out," Brad says. "Instead, it's the beginning of bringing their community together to create even bigger community. And it gets them *started*."

So grab your journal and begin asking yourself a series of questions. "We should write because writing brings clarity and passion to the act of living," Julia Cameron says. "Writing is sensual, experiential, grounding. We should write because writing is good for the soul. We should write because writing yields us a body of work, a felt path through the world we live in." I could not agree more. Get curious about that quiet, insistent voice—the one that's almost a whisper—and then write down the answers. (Turn to "The Lightmaker's Manual" toward the back of the book for a series of prompts that will help you access that whisper.)

By now I have a stack of journals. As I go through them, I can see the evolution of my career, my creativity, and my activism. Through all of the writing and other notes or mementos I've tucked in their pages, I can identify the trajectory I've taken over time. I can follow the trail I've taken to this place, where I am extremely clear on my values and the legacy that I hope my work will leave. I've been able to capture brainstorms and ideas and to map missions and goals.

And it all began by my asking myself those questions all those years ago: *If I didn't practice law, what would I do? How could this provide meaning and purpose to my life? How could I help make the world better?* The process of journaling helped me find the answers, identify all the destinations that lay before me, and determine which of them would fill my life with the most meaning and purpose, while providing an adventure along the way.

All because I listened to the whisper.

PART II

TINDER

The term "tinder" is a large umbrella under which all sorts of materials may be included, but they all have a common purpose: they capture, sustain and transfer that first tiny quantity of heat, whether it comes in the form of a spark or an ember, to the next stage of fuel.

—Daniel Hume, *Fire Making*

When I stand before God at the end of my life, I would hope that I would not have a single bit of talent left, and could say "I used everything you gave me."

—Erma Bombeck

4 | ON SKILLS, GIFTS, AND BECOMING A TRUSTEE

Several years ago, I was invited to give the closing keynote at a leadership conference hosted by a university. The conference was intended for the school's business students, and the theme for the event was "Be the Change," based on that famous quotation by Mahatma Gandhi: "Be the change you wish to see in the world." It was an honor to be invited to speak. At that point, I'd never spoken at a university before, and I looked forward to meeting the students. But I was keenly anticipating the event for another reason: the lunchtime keynote speaker was Arun Gandhi, grandson of the Mahatma.

Arun Gandhi, an activist in his own right, was born and grew up in apartheid-era South Africa. Life under the apartheid regime was exceedingly difficult, and as he tells it, as a child he was constantly getting into fights: the Black kids didn't like him because he wasn't Black, and the white folks didn't like him because he clearly wasn't white. After he had gotten into tons of bloody scuffles, his parents decided to send him back to India to live with his grandfather, who was rising to the height of his popularity. (Would that we *all* could send our difficult children to Grandpa Gandhi when they got out of hand.) While living with his grandfather, Mr. Gandhi continued his regular schooling, but he was also educated in the ways of peace and nonviolence and in the activist work that he continues to this day.

The day before the conference, I drove the two-and-a-half hours to Nacogdoches, Texas. The event began bright and early the following day on the Stephen F. Austin State University campus, so that morning I woke up just after sunrise, showered and dressed, and checked out of the hotel in preparation to meet the shuttle that would take me to the event. While I was at the front desk waiting for the busy clerk to finish up, I spotted Mr. Gandhi sitting in the lobby, having a quiet cup of tea. Our eyes met, and I smiled. He must have recognized me from the conference marketing materials, because he smiled back. And then, improbably, with one hand he graciously gestured to the empty seat next to him.

"You may join me," he said.

It is a deeply held tenet of mine that when any member of Mahatma Gandhi's family invites me to join them for tea, I accept. So I finished with the clerk, grabbed a mug from the coffee bar, and sat next to him, introducing myself. Then, to my own horror, I spent the next thirty minutes shamelessly peppering him with the sorts of questions that I'm sure he is asked all the time and is tired of answering. But he was totally gracious, telling me all about his childhood, what he valued most about his time with the Mahatma, and the work he was currently doing. The shuttle bus arrived to take us to campus far sooner than I would have liked.

That conversation remains one of the most meaningful times of my life. I especially cherish the moment when he shared with me (and later with the students at the conference) his grandfather's concept of *trusteeship*. According to Mr. Gandhi, the Mahatma said we all have talents and skills and gifts, and we mistakenly get our egos tied up in them. We think we own them, and we believe they provide our measure of worthiness in the world. But the Mahatma believed that these skills and talents and gifts are merely given to us in *trusteeship*—for care and use, certainly, but not ownership. God, or Allah, or the universe—or whatever higher power you might believe in—grants them to us to hold and to use during our time on this earth, to make the world better and brighter and more con-nected. That, Mr. Gandhi said, is the true meaning of life.

I love this idea that our gifts are entrusted to us, not for our own edification but for use for the benefit of others. There's just one hitch: How do you figure out what your gifts actually *are*?

The good news is that the process of understanding your gifts and their value is similar to choosing the issues around which you want to advocate: you pay attention.

My friend Mira Jacob is a gifted writer. Her critically acclaimed debut novel, *The Sleepwalker's Guide to Dancing*, was named one of the best books of 2014 by *Kirkus Reviews*, the *Boston Globe*, Good-reads, and Bustle, just to name a few. All of these accolades are well-deserved—it's a brilliant book.

But Mira has the soul of an activist, and for her sophomore effort, she did a complete one-eighty: she *drew* a graphic memoir. In *Good Talk: A Memoir in Conversations*, Mira draws and writes about her childhood growing up as one of the very few South Asians in New Mexico, as well as what it is like being in a mixed-race marriage and raising a biracial son in a post-9/11 world. She tells personal stories that cause readers to both nod and squirm with recognition, all while igniting curiosity and empathy.

I have bought and given away more copies of this book than I can count. The way Mira tackles racism, colorism, nationalism, immigration, LGBTQ+ issues, and so much more is nothing short of revelatory and revolutionary. And I'm not the only one who thinks this: *Good Talk* was shortlisted for the National Book Critics Circle Award, longlisted for the PEN Open Book Award, named a *New York Times* Notable Book, and acclaimed as a best book of the year by *Time, Esquire, Publisher's Weekly*, and *Library Journal*. It was even nominated for an Eisner Award, the organization that awards creative achievement in American comic books and is sort of the Academy Awards for the comic industry.

What makes this even *more* amazing? *Good Talk* was the first time Mira had ever drawn anything for public consumption.

I've known Mira for years, and I remember being stunned when she announced that she'd be creating a graphic memoir. I'd always known Mira as a novelist. "I had no idea you were such a gifted artist," I remember telling her.

She laughed. "It's very funny," she said. "Whenever someone says, 'You're an artist?' I want to giggle and say 'No, I just draw things.'"

I smiled. "There's a difference?"

"Honestly, I don't actually know what the distinction is in my head, except one of those things comes with flowing robes and long wine lunches, and the other is me, doodling on a computer."

I was incredulous that she didn't recognize her own talent. She continued, "I know. A friend of mine who *is* an artist, said, 'You will *have* to get over this.' I was like, 'Yeah, just give me seven more glasses of wine and I'll start saying I'm an artist!'"

I laughed, but I didn't let it go. Given that she didn't consider herself an artist, why would she believe she was capable of drawing a graphic memoir?

"Well," she began slowly, "If I'm honest, I've *always* drawn. Drawing has always been an outlet for me. I drew all through *Sleepwalker's*

Guide. Whenever I couldn't get a scene to work out, I'd choose an object from that scene and draw it so that I could think. Drawing is a bit of a relaxation tool for me."

She paused for a long moment. And then she spoke softly, almost conspiratorially: "So I'll tell you two things that happened with this book, that allowed me to dare to create it. The first is something a friend of mine told me that made a huge impression on me. After *Sleepwalker's Guide* came out, I went on a book tour, and of course I met many people who had read the book. A lot of those people felt really passionately about it, which was an incredible feeling. But the truth is, it's also a terrifying feeling."

"Terrifying?" I was confused. "Why?"

Frustration shadowed her face. "Because the question everyone kept asking was, 'Is there a sequel? I want a sequel. I want the sequel to be about *this*. Tell me more about the sequel.'" Mira sighed. "There was this assumption that these characters would live on forever, and at that point I knew for sure there was no sequel, and how could there ever be? I knew that it ended where it needed to end."

"So I was talking to this friend who's an architect, and like everyone, he said to me, 'What are you thinking for the next book?' And I just sort of burst out, 'I don't *know!* Because all anyone wants is a sequel!'"

Mira's architect friend looked at her in silence for a moment. Then he said, "You know what I like to do when I'm thinking of starting a new project? I like to think of what's possible as if it were a topographic map. And then I ask myself, 'Where have I never been before?'"

"Whoa," I breathed, as Mira paused in her story.

"I know, right?" Mira picked up steam. "As soon as he said that, I instantly saw a topographic map of New Mexico, since I'm so bound to that place in my soul. I repeated to myself, 'Where have I never been? Where have I never been?' And suddenly, I knew where I had never been—but also, where I had *always* been: in this world where I draw things and then I write them."

Soon after that Mira called her agent, who had always been supportive of her work. She began, "You know these drawings I've been doing—?"

Mira grinned at the memory. "Before I could even finish the thought, she interrupted me. 'Yeah, you should draw a book.'"

"You're kidding!"

"Karen, she said it so quickly. She didn't even stop to think about it. And then she said, 'You know, you always draw, and you send me your drawings all year long. You really should draw a book.' I was so surprised that I almost didn't believe her. I asked, 'Are you *really* on board?' And she just insisted: 'No, *really: you should draw a book.*' She was 1,000 percent behind it."

At this, Mira paused, and took a deep breath before speaking again.

"Then the other thing that happened, Karen, was what was going on in 2014. As you know, I'm in a mixed-race family—I'm Indian American, my husband is Jewish American, and our son looks more like me. Back then, he was starting to figure out his skin color, and really what *our* skin color meant in terms of our lives, which is a crazy thing for a six-year-old to be grappling with. At the same time, he developed an *enormous* Michael Jackson obsession. And then, on top of all of this, Ferguson erupted."

The fatal shooting of unarmed Black teenager Michael Brown by white police officer Darren Wilson in Ferguson, Missouri, launched nationwide fury and grief. The protests were part of Black Lives Matter, a decentralized movement that advocates nonviolent action against police brutality and racially motivated violence. Mira's brow furrowed at the memory.

"All of these things were coming together and he and I were having the craziest conversations," continued Mira. "It was painful. And I remember trying to write a think piece about everything that was going on, but the problem with think pieces in America at that moment was that any sentence that was constructed around a person's opinions about what was happening was dismissed. And listen: I have been in this America for many decades as a brown woman, so I am very familiar with all the outright and subtle dismissals."

So rather than write a think piece, Mira decided to write and draw the conversations that were happening around her. "Because people can have any feelings they want about my opinions, but they can't dismiss the conversations that were actually happening in my own life," she explained. "They witness the conversations, and then they have to grapple with their own feelings. That's how I ended up writing and drawing a piece about the conversations that were happening at that time, and it was eventually published on BuzzFeed. It's called '37 Difficult Questions from My Mixed-Race Son.' And that became the basis of *Good Talk*."

What's so amazing about Mira's story is the way her innate gifts intersected with her inner whisper, calling on her to comment on the racism and bigotry that were swirling around her. The question she asked herself, suggested by her architect friend—Where haven't I been before?—opened her mind to new horizons. Her gifts of writing, drawing, and communication illuminated a possibility of a whole new genre of expression for her: a graphic memoir. And thank heavens: because of her willingness to use these gifts, she created a book that now consistently tops "must read" lists for folks interested in learning more about racism and other types of bigotry and who want to be allies and accomplices in the eradication of discrimination. Those skills that light her up—writing, drawing, and communication—were gifts that, as Mr. Gandhi described, had been placed in her trusteeship.

She was using them to make light and change the world.

◆ ◆ ◆

Naming our gifts and establishing how to use them as advocacy tools don't come as naturally for some of us as it did for Mira. On that fateful day when I cracked open my journal after my run-in with my coworker, I was truly at a loss. What would the future hold for me? How could I possibly contribute to making the world better?

Also, I was terrified. At the time, I had been practicing law for about fourteen years, and even though the job was highly stressful, the truth is that *at least I knew what I was doing.* There's a certain comfort in knowing your way around a gig and being able to do it on autopilot—even if you wake up every morning with dread about going to do it.

Furthermore, I was tinkering with doing something that I had never before dreamed of: quitting my job with absolutely no plan of what to do next. This would be the foolhardiest decision that I had ever made; I'd never quit *anything* without a plan. But I knew it was time for a change, and not only because of a hostile coworker. I was experiencing strange bouts of heart palpitations, even when lying quietly in bed, and these panic attacks were occurring more and more frequently. I knew I needed to leave the practice of law sooner rather than later. But to do *what*, exactly? What was I good at? What did I love? What gifts had been placed in my trusteeship?

So one of those mornings, in frustration, my analytical mind took over. I grabbed my journal once again and this time, I made a list of everything—and I mean *everything*—that I enjoyed doing.

I figured that if I spent some time doing so, perhaps I could really nail down what makes me tick.

The first item on my list was *blogging*. This came easily: I had been actively keeping a blog for several years by then and had developed a considerable following. I loved using my site as a way to connect with people and share stories. Oh, and images—so I quickly added *photography* as the second item. Easy enough. Then I really started thinking.

Because my career had prompted this introspection in the first place, I tried to think of anything that I enjoyed about my law job. What did a *good* day at my job look like? The first thing that popped into my head were the days when people pretty much left me alone, I had few meetings, and I spent my day writing a contract from scratch. So I wrote down on my list: *writing contracts in solitude*.

I stared at the page. There was something sort of sad about this—and not just because it confirmed that I was a nerdy hermit. In the moment, it was hard to see how writing contracts was going to add meaning to my life, far less change the world. Was this really what I was destined to do?

Nonetheless, I wrote it down and pressed on. What else did I like about my work? I started thinking that back when I was the chief of staff of a large Fortune 200 company, I enjoyed putting together PowerPoint presentations for my boss, the CEO. I wrote down *creating presentations*.

Again, my inner critic had something to say—I mean, it's not like PowerPoint has ever been hailed as a tool of the revolution. But again I pushed through and kept writing, eventually also adding things that I loved about my nonwork life. *Public speaking. Helping people problem-solve. Traveling.* Each time I wrote something down, my inner critic spoke up. But I kept going, and eventually the voice got quieter. Before I knew it, an hour had passed.

The list was long, and it was ridiculous. In addition to arguably practical activities like *reading books* and *writing contracts*, my list included things like *roller skating, hanging out on the beach, dancing alone in my bedroom, drinking tea*, and of course, *singing in the shower*.

I sat there for a moment and stared at the list. It was clear that this "love list" contained items that brought me considerable joy, but honestly, the only question that came to my mind at that moment was *why? Why* did I like going to the movies? Or traveling? Or eating good food?

I went through each item and wrote down what it was that I liked about doing those things.

Why did I like singing in the shower? Because I love expressing myself without censorship or worrying if people will laugh at me.

Why did I enjoy dancing by myself? Same reason.

Drinking tea? I love the flavor of tea, of course, but I also love watching it steep. I love watching the milk slowly stir into the tea and make the liquid a lighter, more opaque brown.

Each time I came up with a reason for liking one of the items on my love list, I would add the reason as a new item on my list:

I love the feeling of expressing myself without self-censorship.
I love watching the milk slowly stir into tea and the transformation that follows.
I love to visit new cultures, try new foods, meet new people.
I love watching the colors of the ocean, how they change as
it gets later in the day.

I began to realize that some of the reasons that I enjoy an activity might be completely different from the reasons someone else enjoys the same activity. For example, some people enjoy books because they like how reading transports them to another place and time; I actually enjoy studying how different authors use language and turn a phrase.

And I was starting to see patterns emerge. Blogging, writing contracts, journaling, and reading books: all are related to *written expression*. Photography, traveling, and yes, even pouring Elmer's glue on the palm of my hand, letting it dry, and peeling it off (I told you this list was ridiculous): these all relate to *communication* and *visual expression*. Giving talks at conferences, reading out loud to my daughter, and even creating elaborate and animated PowerPoint presentations: all connect to a love of *public speaking*.

Over and over again, as I went down my list, I watched as certain items found themselves in one of those categories. There were other categories too, of course: my love of cooking Trinidadian food, drinking a good rum, blogging, and helping people problem-solve had to do with making connections. Looking at travel magazines, scuba diving, and trying new cuisines all related to my craving for adventure. But overwhelmingly, most of the items on my list could be categorized under those first three headings: speaking out loud, writing for expression, and creating visual inspiration and communication.

I love to speak, I love to write, I love to shoot.

Speak, write, shoot.

I call these three words—these activities that light me up, from the inside of my soul—my light words. These are the activities I know I'll do for the rest of my life because they bring me joy. These are the gifts Mr. Gandhi was talking about—the talents that I hold in trusteeship. (Incidentally, don't miss the exercise included in "The Lightmaker's Manual" toward the back of this book to help you find your own light words.)

Since naming these light words, I've come to realize that these gifts and skills are what I take with me—just as Mira takes writing, drawing, and communicating with her—on my journey to make the world better. I think about these three words constantly as I look for opportunities to serve or advocate, intent on using them as tools. Ideally, I get to do all three at the same time, if I can. I mean, if I'm wired to light up when I do these things, I owe it to myself—and to the world—to make them happen as often as possible.

So I do.

And I've never looked back.

5 | ON INTEGRITY, EMPATHY, AND KINDNESS AS RESISTANCE

In early 2004, my husband and I were awaiting the birth of our daughter. Well into our adoption process, we had already been matched with her birth mother and had even attended a few of her prenatal doctor's visits. We were excited but also terrified: we'd only decided to adopt a few months earlier, and even though we were sure we were making the right decision, it was rapidly becoming very clear that we knew nothing about what it took to parent. The baby was due in mere weeks, so we needed to figure it out—and fast.

One night when I was googling "how to be a mother" or something equally panicky, I stumbled upon a site unlike anything I'd seen before. It was an online diary—a "weblog," as it was called then—chronicling the day-to-day life of a mother and her young family. It was funny and personal, and the woman behind it, Megan Morrone, had even included a way to contact her via email. *Keeping an online diary like this could be great for keeping our families up to date with our adoption process*, I thought. Since Marcus and I are both immigrants, it was always a challenge to keep up with our families in England and Trinidad, respectively. With something like this, they could just log in and read our latest entries. I decided to reach out to Megan. "How are you making the internet do that?" I asked. "I think I want to do that too."

Megan couldn't have been more lovely. It turns out that she was a professional technology writer enthralled with this new web platform. She gave me a few pointers, and within a few days, I had my own blog. Chookooloonks.com was officially born.

I can't stress enough how early in blogging this was. Facebook was merely weeks old and still only intended for use by Harvard University students. Twitter was nonexistent, to say nothing of Snapchat, TikTok, or any of the other myriad of social media apps around at the time of this writing. I didn't know a soul in my day-to-day life who even knew what a blog *was*, much less had one of their own. In my circle of friends, I was charting new territory, and I expect other bloggers who began their blogs around the same time felt the same way. There were no such things as influencers, or monetization, or even a Kardashian (unless you were talking about O. J. Simpson's defense attorney). We bloggers were enthralled by the democratization of the internet: prior to this, the web had been solely the purview of corporations. The idea that individuals could write and express and *publish* their thoughts—almost like Erma Bombeck! Or Dave Barry!—was exciting and empowering. What we wrote was pretty true to who we were. Sure, we might have been more sarcastic online than in real life, or even more sweet-natured, but we were mostly honest. You could assume that if you met us in real life, you wouldn't find us espousing thoughts or ideologies that were any different from what we'd written online. For the most part, back in those early days, we didn't lie.

Years passed, and I kept at my blog: sharing stories of adoption, new motherhood, and then over time switching to sharing photographs with accompanying commentary on my life. Others kept at it, too, and eventually, blogging became big business. Honestly, it was incredibly exciting: people who didn't have careers before their blogs were suddenly making big money; those who *did* have careers were discovering new opportunities that might even be more fulfilling than their current jobs. A few bloggers become *New York Times* bestselling authors or multimillionaire business owners. But blogs also helped some folks, like me, become activists. Given that we were writing about the issues that were important to us, people who were similarly passionate about adoption or the environment or education reform or civil rights or a myriad of other topics would share and amplify our voices. And suddenly, we found ourselves influential advocates for diverse causes around the world.

But somewhere along the way, as all this growth was happening, bloggers—and later, YouTubers, Instagrammers, Facebookers, and other social media influencers—began writing content solely to please their audiences. I certainly wasn't immune to this trend, as I was paying attention to which posts seemed to garner the most conversation and the most praise. We all began curating our feeds more carefully, with beautiful, perfect images that helped to attract more attention.

Ironically, during this time, "how to be authentic" became a huge topic of conversation among bloggers. Readers were increasingly asking us how to live authentically in a world of artificiality. Do you see the tension? People wanted "authenticity" online, but folks who were trying to build influence found themselves curating what they shared to appeal to a larger audience. The results were misleading: Were we really supposed to believe that the travel vlogger never experienced jet lag? The food blogger never ruined the soufflé? The design Instagrammer never had a messy home? And the activist on Facebook never experienced moments of doubt?

This tension, by the way, has never left. Since I began blogging more than a decade and a half ago, social media has become so ubiquitous that even casual users are wildly active on all sorts of platforms. I've watched friends of mine suddenly feel pressured to show only autotuned, Photoshopped images of themselves, their partners, their kids, and their lifestyles—and then grapple with the discomfort that they're leaving friends and family with false impressions. Their lives contain more anger, sadness, or heartbreak than they are letting on, and as a result, they feel dishonest or duplicitous. This tension is only exacerbated when they find themselves ignited by an issue or injustice about which they can no longer remain silent. When they express this distress online, they're met with comments like, "I had no idea you were such an angry person," or "I'm so disappointed that you feel this way," or perhaps the most dismissive and belittling: "I'm only here for your kids' cute pictures [or cool recipes or funny life commentary]. Stick to that. Ditch the politics."

Given all this, the word *authenticity* has lost some of its meaning. Authenticity, at least when it comes to online expression, seems to have morphed to mean "airbrushed reality" or, even more horrifying, oversharing. So as I've entered more and more into an activism space with my work, I've come to value a higher standard than authenticity. Instead, I try to go for *integrity*.

Integrity is much larger than authenticity; it encompasses trustworthiness. It implies a moral code. It doesn't have the airbrushedness (or worse, the bare-it-all-ness) that "authenticity" often connotes; rather, it inspires an adherence to a moral code. I think integrity challenges us more than authenticity does, because it requires us to be mindful of our best selves. It's less about how others perceive us and far more about how we think of ourselves. And when it comes to activism, integrity calls for us to stand our ground about what we believe.

This may sound easy, but it can be the hardest part of activism. Integrity means staying the course even when it seems like things aren't getting better. Integrity means resisting the urge to copy others who make advocacy look easy, and it means forging your own path with your own skills and gifts, whether others find it entertaining or not. And sometimes integrity means speaking up for justice, even though you might lose friends and family members as a result.

◆ ◆ ◆

Integrity will almost always include an interplay of both courage and vulnerability. I'm lucky to have a close friend who not only fiercely models integrity in her own life, both online and off, but who has built much of her internationally renowned work around it.

Brené Brown and I have been friends for more than a decade; I met her when, in her words, she was "just a girl with a book and a blog." A research professor at the University of Houston, Brené has spent over two decades studying courage, vulnerability, shame, and empathy. She exploded to global prominence when her TED talk, "The Power of Vulnerability," became a viral sensation. Since 2010, when it was first published, it has been viewed almost fifty million times. In the decade that followed, Brené has published several number one *New York Times* bestsellers, starred in her own Netflix special about her research, and even had a cameo in a movie created by and starring Amy Poehler, a huge fan of her work. Through it all, Brené has remained a fierce friend, one who is rock solid in her own values and what she stands for.

Brené's work is quoted constantly by devoted fans, but one in particular that appears all over the internet is about integrity. "Integrity is choosing courage over comfort," she says. "It's choosing what's right over what is fun, fast, or easy. It's choosing to practice your values, rather than simply professing them." This is a pretty profound statement, and while it's easy to quote, it's much harder to practice. But Brené lives it. In recent years, I've watched my friend wade into activism on behalf of Black Lives Matter and LGBTQ+ issues and to speak up loudly against discrimination in all its forms. Given her meteoric success, I've wondered if she has ever worried about how much she has to lose. Her unwavering commitment to equality and belonging could quite literally alienate a considerable percentage of the people who have loved her work.

Because we live in the same city, whenever Brené and I get together, it's usually for a long walk. But for this conversation, given the trajectory of the COVID-19 pandemic at the time, we decided that the safest way to connect was through videoconferencing. We quickly caught up on our families and personal news before getting to the reason why I'd called.

"By all accounts, you've made it," I began. "You've got a really successful career, and it's been such a personal joy to watch your work evolve. But I've noticed that in recent years, you've been really taking on racism and other types of discrimination and doing so in ways that look really brave to me. Having lived as a Black woman and an immigrant in this country, I know these are conversations most people are *really* uncomfortable having, so I imagine it takes some serious courage for you to even broach the subjects. Why even take the issue on?"

She thought for a minute. "It's interesting; I haven't really talked about this." She thought for a moment longer, and then started speaking slowly. "This is a brand-new aha for me: I think the reason my work resonates so much is because it's not the work itself that people are drawn to. People are actually drawn to watching me *struggle* with the work. I'm like, 'Here's what the research says, and it's messed up and I don't want to do it either, but here's how I'm trying and failing, and trying and failing.' *That's* what people want to watch. If I were unwilling to take on hard topics because I can't do them perfectly, that would bankrupt the entire premise of my work."

I smiled, but I wasn't convinced. I pushed harder: "I mean, I get that. But here's the thing: *no one would have to know.* You could simply continue talking about courage and shame—hard topics in and of themselves—and never actually say much of anything about racism or bigotry or discrimination, without anyone being any the wiser."

She frowned. "But *I* would know," she responded, as if it were silly to even suggest otherwise. "Besides, this is who I am. This isn't new: I've been studying discrimination and oppression for a long time. Remember, I have a bachelor's degree, master's degree, and a doctorate in social work. Over the course of my education, I've taken classes on racial discrimination. I've taken classes on systemic oppression. I came to the University of Houston to do my education and remained because U of H had the only graduate social work program with a political concentration in the nation. I wrote papers on white supremacy twenty years ago. My very first book, the one I self-published, talks about privilege and shame."

I nodded slowly, thinking about all the books she has written that I own and have read. "Honestly, I hadn't thought about how much social work would necessarily require study in those topics," I said.

"Right," she smiled. "So I've put out this big body of work, and people have attached to it and made it what they needed to be. And the majority of the followers of my work—mostly white women—need my work on courage to be soulful and spiritual. So when I call on my education and say something like, 'The system's not broken; it's working just like we designed it—and by *we*, I mean white people,' they're immediately put off. They're like, 'Oh, no, no, no, don't talk about that.'"

She became even more passionate. "But honestly, Karen, if people choose not to examine the part of my work that talks about barriers to belonging, or skipped those pages in my books, then they don't know my work as a whole. Because of my research and education, there *is* no work on courage and empathy and belonging without also tackling racism or discrimination or other issues of disenfranchisement. Those are the bones of the work. *Dehumanization is the bones of the work.* How could I *not* weigh in on hard conversations about those topics?"

At this, her eyes narrowed. "You say my tackling this is brave, but let's never forget: I can wade in these conversations, be perceived as brave, and then return to a white life of relative safety and privilege. That's not bravery. That's not courage. That's just doing the right thing. And if we've gotten to the point in this world that doing the right thing is seen as 'heroic'? Well . . ." she inhaled slowly. "That's an effin' nightmare."

I suspect that Brené's ease with tackling difficult subjects is grounded in the fact that she has been practicing courage for a long time now. According to her research, the intensely uncomfortable feeling of vulnerability is the greatest measure of courage that we have. In fact, she maintains that there isn't any courage without vulnerability, because they are inextricably linked. Activism, while often clearly viewed as "the right thing," involves a heaping helping of vulnerability as well. It's scary to stick your neck out for a cause when the entire world seems to be arguing for the opposite. It's all well and good to get loud about the things that are important to you; that said, it stands to reason that to do that well, vulnerability and courage need to come along for the ride.

So this begs the question, *How* do we cultivate courage? Ultimately, courage is a practice, one we must keep returning to. As Brené would say, we don't have to be perfect—just engaged and committed to aligning our values with our actions. "I have this motto when I'm in hard conversations," she told me. "I say, *I'm here to get it right, not to be right.* I just repeat that over and over again. I'm here to learn and evolve, not to win arguments. So, if you think about it, it's nuts: I've got those degrees and probably thirty hours of graduate-level courses on oppression, racism, and systemic problems, and I *still* have to have crazy practices to stay in awareness about what's happening." She sighed. "No one said this was easy."

That's a fact. As I've watched Brené navigate her own activism journey, she has taught me that cultivating courage requires becoming clear—and I mean *crystal* clear—about our values. When we can name and stay rooted in our values, then doing the right thing suddenly doesn't feel so much "brave," as Brené says, as it does simply "the only way forward." (And if you're wondering what your own core values are, keep reading. Chapter 6 and the journaling exercises in "The Lightmaker's Manual" toward the back of this book will help you identify and name them.)

Values, it turns out, light our way.

Perhaps by now you have identified the skills and talents that light you up and that can be used as tools to create positive change. If so, congratulations! You have almost everything you need to enter into the activism fray in a way that avoids burnout and allows you to tap into your own joyful soul. There are, however, three additional traits that kept emerging from my interviews with the diverse lightmakers who appear in this book.

Almost to a person, each activist I spoke to maintained that empathy, compassion, and kindness were paramount in their advocacy work. In my own life, I've learned that empathy and compassion are core elements not only of good activism but also—somewhat selfishly—of joy and well-being for me. "I know that each time I have acted compassionately, I have experienced a joy in me that I find in nothing else," Archbishop Tutu says in *The Book of Joy*. "And even the cynic will have to admit that this is how we are wired. We're wired to be other-regarding."

This "wiring" toward others—and indeed, the importance of empathy and compassion in advocacy—became even more clear when I spoke with activist and artist Jordan Seaberry. As a self-described "painter by night, public policy director by day," Jordan's Instagram feed is filled with vibrant colors and textures of his multimedia works, many of which are focused on anti-racism. He was born and raised in Chicago and is a graduate of the prestigious Rhode Island School of Design. His work is in galleries and collections around the country, and one of his largest works is even owned by Michelle Alexander, author of the seminal book on race and mass incarceration, *The New Jim Crow*.

In addition to the gorgeous portfolio of art he has created, Jordan is also the director of public policy and advocacy at the Nonviolence Institute in Providence, an organization whose mission is "to teach, by word and example, the principles of nonviolence." The organization works tirelessly to reduce gun and other types of violence in the city through education, public policy and advocacy initiatives, and support and resources for individuals directly impacted by violence.

Jordan is a thoughtful man with an easy smile. As we talked, he exhibited a quiet passion for both his art and his activism. Which came first for him, I asked: art or activism?

"Oh, art," he said, without hesitation. "Most people assume advocacy brought me to art, but it's definitely the other way around. To my mind, advocacy is a way of thinking creatively and a way of living artistically. They both feel really true for me."

Jordan began creating art as a child, when his mother bought him a set of oil paints so he could paint along with the famed television art instructor Bob Ross. "My best friend Mike would come over, and he'd sit on the bed and read comic books, while I had my canvas in front of the TV and I painted." He smiled at the memory. "You know, my mom didn't really have extra money to spend on a whim, but she saw that I was interested in art, so she went out and got that Bob Ross paint set, a canvas, and a little easel. She had no way of knowing that, however many decades later, I would be doing this seriously and professionally. But she saw that I had a passion for it. And she cleared the runway for me to follow that path."

We eventually began talking about activism, and Jordan became more animated as he shared his philosophy on the subject, believing it to be broader than simply protesting. In his mind, activism can be divided into two realms: *mobilizing*, under which more traditional forms of protest would lie, and *organizing*, which is something bigger. "I think it's easy for a lot of folks to confuse organizing and mobilizing," he explained. "With mobilization, the point is simply to get the idea out front: you need bodies on the line, for example. Or you need folks to show up at the rally. And mobilization is important, in that you're amplifying a call and the point is clear and yelled and demonstrated."

Organizing, on the other hand, isn't just mobilizing, Jordan said: "It's *changing minds*. And that requires the deepest type of listening, and the deepest type of understanding and compassion, because each person approaches issues and ideas differently, and you need to strive to understand in order to know how to shift mindsets."

In other words, mobilizing is about getting folks to show up for an event or a campaign or a protest; organizing is about creating lasting change.

Jordan's work with the Nonviolence Institute focuses on violence reduction and prisoners' rights, as well as helping the formerly incarcerated reintegrate into society. I asked him how he got into advocacy in the first place—whether he'd been an activist in college, and what form it took—and he described a time in his early twenties, one that quickly makes evident how he can tap so deeply into empathy as he connects with the clients he serves. As a relatively new student at the Rhode Island School of Design, Jordan became deeply disillusioned by the profound racial and wealth disparity between some of his classmates and many of the local citizens of Providence.

"Coming from the South Side of Chicago where I attended a public high school, and going straight from there to RISD, was just such a culture shock for me," he explained. "Not just racially, which was most obvious, but also economically. There were levels of wealth and disparities in class that I'd never experienced before. My family was solidly middle class, my parents were married, we didn't move during my childhood, and we owned our home: when I was coming up, I always felt really, really privileged. But then I got to RISD and realized that I didn't know the half of it! I was in class with the heirs to fortunes of millionaire and celebrity artists."

He frowned. "And I also came to realize that Providence is actually not a college town, but a city that actually has a lot in common with Chicago. A lot of the same issues that exist in Chicago—in terms of policing, poverty, housing instability, and economic uncertainty—exist in this community, though admittedly on a smaller scale. And that, to me, felt like a calling."

His activism began slowly, Jordan told me. He grinned. "My friends and I started a food distribution program when I was still at RISD. At the time, the school had a meal plan policy where you could save up your meals and cash them out on one day. I was a real scrawny kid and I didn't eat all that much, so I would always have ten or so leftover meals at the end of the week. I'd cash them all out and I'd walk out with a box of food. I'd go down to the downtown center, and just pass it out to whoever wanted it. I realized that I had the privilege of having a cafeteria with tons of food in it that was going to go to waste if I didn't cash those meals out. And I knew the city had people who looked like me, who I cared about, who I loved and felt some kinship with, who were going hungry. I felt a responsibility to put some of that privilege in action."

Still, despite his efforts to make a difference, the disparity between the vulnerable citizens of Providence and his wealthy classmates haunted him. He became so unhappy, in fact, that he ended up dropping out of school. As a result, he lost his on-campus housing and job, and for ten months he was homeless, living out of his car.

"It was a really hard time, and a really sad time." His brow furrowed. "You know, I remember nights when it was snowing, and I couldn't open the car door, because there was snow up the side. So I'd just have to spend the day in the car or sleeping at the Kmart. I remember the security guard coming up and knocking on the window—not even being mean or harassing but just saying, 'Hey, you can't sleep here.' You know, it felt so . . ." He fell silent. Then he said, "I wondered if there would ever be a moment where I wouldn't feel quite so alone."

I shuddered, imagining the loneliness and the cold.

Jordan's face soon brightened. "But I remember the first step to getting back on my feet: I had a job interview at a place called the Center for Dynamic Learning. I found the job on Craigslist, I think. I walked into the interview wearing the best shirt that I owned, but it was wrinkled and it was unclean." He smiled as he shook his head.

"I did my best, but I knew that I didn't look the way a job applicant is expected to look. But even so, they gave me a shot. They took a chance on me. They saw something in me that I certainly couldn't have seen in myself at the time. And to this day, the woman who gave me that job—Beth Cunha—is still a good friend of mine, and we talk all the time. She's been a guiding light for me."

What an incredible story, I thought. I took a deep breath. "I have to think that this experience—enduring homelessness, being given a chance—must give you so much empathy for the people you work with now."

"I hope so." He nodded with emphasis. "Not only because, in a sense, I've experienced a little bit more than many other folks who enter activism, but also because I think a lot of people who meet me today would never suspect I have that story in my past. I try to approach everyone knowing that there are pieces of *their* story that I don't know and won't *ever* know. But if you think about it, empathy is actually tied up in that unknowing. We don't have to know everyone's story to love them."

Jordan is right, of course: you can feel love, in the form of compassion and empathy, for all people, even (and perhaps especially) for those whose stories you don't yet know. Feeling this love is often easy when you're advocating on behalf of a community; it may be much harder when you're debating someone who holds an opposing view. Regardless, in all aspects of activism, compassion and empathy are superpowers. And the way that empathy and compassion usually manifest themselves is through kindness.

◆ ◆ ◆

Kindness—acting with generosity, consideration, or concern for others—can be one of the most difficult and challenging aspects in activism. When we face an opinion or action that opposes our beliefs or challenges our values, acting with kindness is often the last thing we want to do. Think about the last time you were on social media. Did you see people—who in real life seem like perfectly reasonable, even-tempered folks—lash out at nameless others who believe something different? Did you see comments that resorted to name-calling? And let's be honest: if you happened to be one of those nameless folks being targeted by that person's opinion, your knee-jerk reaction might have been to lash back.

Yet any satisfaction gained from having a sharp, hot-tempered response—even in the face of true injustice—can be relatively short-lived. Even when I am certain my anger is justified, if I channel that anger into meanness or some other churlish response, I can't help but feel a pang of regret that I've allowed that person to force me onto the low road. Make no mistake: I am pro-anger. I find it an incredibly motivating emotion. Yet anger, left unfettered, can be incredibly corrosive, and lead to unthinking actions you later regret. It's like the writer George Saunders said in his 2013 commencement speech at Syracuse University: "Here's something I know to be true," he said. "Although it's a little corny, and I don't quite know what to do with it: what I regret most in my life are *failures of kindness.*"

When it comes to kindness in activism, I know no kinder person in the world than my friend, activist and lightmaker Asha Dornfest. In addition to being one of my closest friends, Asha is a writer and an organizer, with the gift of creating amazing communities designed to support and uplift each other. Years ago she founded Parent Hacks, a community of parents who, through the sharing of their own experiences, helped each other navigate the often difficult and stressful world of young parenthood. More recently she has collaborated to organize more than seven thousand people in her hometown of Portland, Oregon, to actively resist xenophobic, racist, misogynistic, ableist, anti-LGBTQ+, anti-Muslim, anti-Semitic, and anti-Earth policies.

Even though Asha says she is occasionally motivated by anger—and maybe even fury—she is never cruel or mean-spirited, nor does she ever appear to succumb to her ire. No matter who she is speaking to, she is always unfailingly gracious and humane. Since graciousness in the face of opposition isn't one of my gifts (to say the least), I asked her how she manages to do so.

"When it comes to activism, I actually like to use the word *invitation*," she explained. "In the traditional model of activism, people think of opposing positions as, say, two different teams. So imagine there's a line in between the teams, like in a game of tug-of-war, except instead of a rope, they're competing over a specific issue. Each team is pulling the rope, or issue, and like in tug-of-war, the goal is to get as many people on your side as possible. Of course, if you pull hard enough, their team will fall over, and you win, right?"

"Right," I nodded.

"Right," Asha nodded:

Except I hate tug-of-war! I never wanted to play that game when I was a kid, and I've never been interested in pulling people so that they fall over. And for most of the issues we care about, it's possible to approach them in many different ways. You can say, "I have a specific value, and if you share this value, then I invite you to come in and let's talk about this issue. And by talking about it, maybe you'll be inspired to do something differently." And that conversation may inspire someone to take an action, or it may not. But there's no tugging. I'm not yanking anyone into my circle.

I was suspicious. No yanking? Doesn't activism always require convincing the other side, putting on pressure, making demands? Asha appeared to be pointing toward a different posture. Noticing my skepticism, she continued with a grin. "You know how I love a metaphor?" she asked. I grinned back. "So I think of it as a pool of light that I'm inviting someone to step in with me to talk. Or it's like inviting someone up on my porch to talk with me about the things we care about. That's a different kind of activism than most expect, but it's the kind of activism I'm interested in. Because that kind of invitatory activism is not exclusionary. It's not alienating. It's respectful. It's *bigger*."

"Huh," I responded. "I mean, I love this concept, but honestly, I'm not always motivated to be nice."

"Then think of it this way," she said, "being kind is an act of resistance."

I was intrigued. "What does *that* mean?"

"To be clear, I believe in boundaries, and if someone is abusive, I'm not going to sit and take it," she replied. "I'll respectfully end the conversation. But kindness—going into a conversation with a generous assumption of good intent—is, for me, a conscious decision to push against the fact that there are politicians and other people in power who are trying to drive wedges between us. My being kind is a mindful statement saying that I reject intentional manipulation by powerful people who are attempting to turn me into some puppet in their little 'us versus them' war—a war I don't even believe in."

Asha's tone grew firmer. "My intentional kindness is my acting independently, with independent thought. In some ways, it's not even about being nice, or because I'm particularly generous. Being kind is a political statement to actively reject the 'we're right, you're wrong; we're righteous, you're criminals; we're patriotic, you're unpatriotic' construct. I'm just not falling for it."

She took a deep breath. "Besides, Karen, it's just a more prag-matic way to be," she said, calmer now. "If my goal is to bring people with me, I have to start somewhere, and starting by slam-ming the door in someone's face isn't generally going to get what I want. Being kind is a human statement. It's a moral statement. It's an expression of my values. I think that it's so important. It's not because I'm sweet, or nice, or I don't have a temper. This is, ulti-mately, what it means when I say to 'love fiercely.' Kindness is a way to affirm our shared humanity."

Affirming our shared humanity: what a purposeful way to put kind-ness to work as a tool in the often combative world of advocacy. And Brené Brown's research into shame and empathy goes one step further: it proves that being unkind or using shame is antithetical to activism work. "Activism and change require empathy, and here's the truth: shame and empathy do not coexist," Brené explained to me. "What's more, shame is a tool of oppression. Humiliation is a tool of oppression. Belittling is a tool of oppression. Those are *all* tools of oppression. It's like that great Audre Lorde quote: 'We will not dismantle the master's house with the master's tools.' You cannot use tools of oppression to fix oppression."

But before we walk away with the impression that kindness means being accommodating to a fault: there's more. As Brené con-tinued, her eyes narrowed: "Being held accountable for an oppres-sive act and feeling shame is *not* the same thing as *being* shamed. Telling someone that what they did was hurtful or not thoughtful is not *shaming* them. That's simply holding that person account-able. Accountability can be done with kindness and in integrity and is a prerequisite to change. And it is certainly possible to hold someone accountable while staying rooted in values of kindness and compassion."

The ultimate lesson, as we consider the ways in which we'll fight for the causes we believe in, is to firmly do so in a way that does not compromise our integrity. To advocate for others in an honorable way, we need to be able to look at ourselves in the mirror and like who looks back. Staying rooted in our core values is certainly paramount in our activism, but doing so in empathy, compassion, and kindness is what will truly fulfill us. This is true even when it's anger that compels us to action. As Jordan attests, staying in compassion is the source of changing minds (and ultimately policies). To Asha's and Brené's points, kindness itself can be an act of resistance.

The best news? The Dalai Lama and Bishop Tutu affirm that compassion, empathy, and kindness are often sources of joy. "When you show compassion, when you show caring, when you show love to others . . . in a wonderful way you have a deep joy that you can get in no other way," Tutu says. "When you are caring, compassionate, more concerned about the welfare of others than about your own, wonderfully, wonderfully, you suddenly feel a warm glow in your heart."

And that warm glow can be the spark that ignites our own, unique way of making light.

PART III
SPARK

After twenty or so strikes, a tiny wisp of smoke emanated from the little pile; a spark had made a direct hit. Then there was an orange glow as the tinder smoldered and the ember grew. He put it into a bundle of dry honeysuckle bark and blew it into life.

—Daniel Hume, *Fire Making*

I believe that we are all a spark of the divine, and if that spark is nurtured, it can become a burning flame, an eternal force of light.

—John Lewis

6 | ON VALUES, MISSIONS, AND GUITAR STRINGS

Getting clear on your gifts is the first step to creating a light-filled activism practice. But once you've engaged in the introspection required to identify these talents, and once you've committed to kindness and empathy, what then? How do you truly ignite your soulfire by narrowing the issues that will shape the vision for your work?

It helps to actually name your values and declare your mission.

Naming your values isn't as easy as you might think. If I were to give you an exhaustive list of values and ask you to circle the ones that you hold as your own, you might be tempted to circle every one on the list. We like to think that we hold all good values in esteem, but the truth is, only a few are truly core to who we are. I learned this lesson years ago on a magical retreat on the Oregon coast.

One day, while I will still practicing law, I received an invitation from a woman I didn't know personally but whose work I'd followed on her blog. She had also followed mine, which by this point was full of my photography. "I'm inviting a group of creative women to Manzanita, a small town on the Oregon coast," read the email, "and I'd love if you'd join us." The email listed the other women she was inviting, and they were all bloggers whose work I loved. Normally, I never would have accepted the invitation, but it came serendipitously during the time I was considering leaving law, and the idea of spending time in a beautiful setting with creative women seemed like a dream come true. I happily accepted.

We rented a huge house by the sea, and our days were filled with talking about our work, making art, and bonding during long beach walks. The nine women were fine artists, graphic designers, photographers, and authors, and we spent four days together sharing our dreams, encouraging each other in our individual goals, and workshopping challenges we were each facing in our careers. It was during one of these moments that clarity of my own values came.

One of the participants, Andrea Scher, is a photographer and life coach. She was going to be leading a workshop when she returned home to the San Francisco Bay Area, and she wanted to practice an exercise on us. We all gamely agreed, and so she paired us up into four duos and gave us each sheets of paper and a pen. Sitting comfortably on sofas and rugs on the floor, we awaited instructions.

"Okay, first," Andrea began, "at the top of each of the three pages that I gave you, write the names of three people you deeply admire. These could be people you know in real life, like a family member or a friend, or they could be someone famous: a celebrity, a politician, a social leader. You can choose a fictional character, like a person from a movie or a favorite book. You can choose a person who is alive or someone who passed long ago."

At the tops of my three pages, I wrote my maternal grandmother's name, Carmen, Atticus Finch of *To Kill a Mockingbird*, and Barack Obama. Once we'd written our names, we looked at Andrea for our next step.

"Okay, now trade your pages with your partner," she instructed. As we did, she continued, "Take the next thirty minutes to interview each other about why those names made the list: one of you sharing the reasons, and the other taking copious notes. First, one person shares, then at fifteen minutes, the other person should share." I smiled at my partner, a photographer and filmmaker named Alessandra, and we began to share.

Thirty minutes went by quickly, and when Andrea convened us again, she invited us to say what we had written about what our partners had shared. We began taking turns. "She's so loving," one person would say. "He has such a clear sense of justice," said another. As we went around the room, we learned intimate details about why we each loved various family members, celebrities, teachers, and mentors. It was actually surprisingly emotional, and a few tears were shed.

After we were done, Andrea debriefed us. "This is an exercise where we excavated the values that are core to who you are," she said. "We tend to pick our heroes because they reflect back to us the values and beliefs that are most important to who we want to be. So circle the traits that kept coming up when your partner was describing the people on her list. Those traits are the ones she should hold close as she makes decisions and plans for how she'll move through her work and life. Once you're done, hand your notes to your partner."

When I received Alessandra's notes on what I had said about my three heroes, I noticed she had circled phrases like "standing up for what's right," "honesty," and "humor." As I read the words, I realized that these phrases did seem central to who I am and who I want to be. They have helped define the kind of activism I do. And I've kept these values close whenever I've needed to make a difficult decision, or take on a challenging action, especially when I found myself needing to be brave.

Even though we did this exercise in pairs, it's possible to do it on your own, in your journal. I invite you to identify your own core values using the exercise located in the "The Lightmaker's Manual" toward the back of this book. Once you've done so, you're ready for the next step: declaring your mission, which can be critical in illuminating where your activism journey may lead.

◆ ◆ ◆

"Declaring your mission" might sound a bit corporate-y to you, and if so, I hear you. It took me a while to come around to the idea as well. Back in the mid-1980s, my dad was an executive at a large company when corporate mission statements became popular. My father is incredibly passionate about his work, and he thought mission statements were the best invention since pasteurized milk. One weekend morning when I was sixteen, he called my eleven-year-old sister and me into the kitchen and invited us to sit down at the table. We'd never had a "family meeting" before, so my sister and I were a bit suspicious. My mom, who was already in the kitchen, wiped her hands on a dish towel and approached at my dad's request.

Once we were all seated, my father began: "I have decided that we should write a family mission statement."

My sister and I looked at each other, and without a word, got up and walked out of the room. My mom smiled at my dad and patted him sympathetically on the shoulder. Amused, she returned to her dirty dishes.

"What?! It's a good idea!" he called after us plaintively, but no one listened.

As I walked upstairs to my bedroom, I shook my head. A family mission statement was one of the dumbest things my overly keen corporate dad had ever come up with. The idea that the four of us could come up with some mission worth collectively working toward . . . Why? To what end? We weren't a corporation—we were individuals! Sure, we were a family, but that's just a loose collective at best! The idea that we could agree on our joint mission was preposterous. Besides, at sixteen, I had way more important things to think about. Like school. And lip gloss.

And yet . . .

Decades later, I've become a huge champion of personal mission statements—what I have come to call *spark statements*. There's something to be said for spending time figuring out how to declare what you stand for based on your values, and clarifying what you hope your legacy will be. This declaration can serve as a reminder, a guide for your decisions, and a tool to discern which opportunities to accept and which ones to decline. It acts as a spark to ignite your own activism journey. Besides, after doing all the work of taking inventory of your skills and talents and naming your values, you may as well express them all in a succinct manner and in a way that keeps them close.

Still not convinced? It turns out that several of the luminaries I spoke with can easily summarize what they hope the light they create is able to accomplish. My friend Jordan Seaberry, for example, came to understand his own personal mission once he began to align the gifts that he had with purposeful work. After he got that job and moved from homelessness into an apartment, he decided at last to return to the Rhode Island School of Design to finish his degree. He ended up graduating with a bachelor of fine arts degree with honors. Jordan maintains that he excelled in part because he finally had a "tether" to the outside world. He was able to paint all day at the university's studios and then plug into activism in the evenings as he worked for change in Providence. "My paintings began to reflect my living in both worlds—and, for the first time, *loving* both worlds. Because when I was only in the art world, as a new student in design school, I hated it. And when I was only the activism world, I was miserable. But I've now learned that for me, art and activism have to be connected: each is a practice of listening and compassion for the other. Only when I was able to do both could I finally feel like myself."

Listening to this, I asked Jordan if this insight into the interplay of his art and activism allowed him to articulate an overarching personal mission. He didn't even hesitate. "Both my art and my activism are woven into a single desire to connect with the world in a way that is honest and rooted in love," he responded emphatically. "Art is just connection. And organizing is just connection. The foundation of both my art and my activism is definitely that connection, based in love."

A young actor based in Los Angeles, Zuri Adele is part of the ensemble cast of the television show *Good Trouble*. In it, she plays Malika, a Black Lives Matter activist. It's a great character: the writer and showrunner of *Good Trouble* was a fan of Patrisse Cullors, one of the founders of the Black Lives Matter movement. She had read Patrisse's book *When They Call You a Terrorist*, and she was inspired by Patrisse's upbringing and her journey into activism in Los Angeles. Zuri's Malika was inspired by Patrisse's experiences.

As part of the research for her role, Zuri often shadows Patrisse and other leaders of Black Lives Matter, learning from their work and attending protests with them in Los Angeles, and then bringing the experience of that activism to the screen. Jess Weiner, the person who introduced me to Zuri and one of the lightmakers featured in this book, enthused: "Zuri *is* the intersection of joy and activism."

"I call myself a griot," Zuri told me one sunny summer afternoon, on Zoom from her patio swing at home in Los Angeles. She was referring to the storytellers who maintain the tradition of oral history in West Africa. "As an African American woman, I understand and appreciate how so much of our history has been passed down through griots and ritual. So since I use my voice and body to tell as many stories as possible on screen and on stages, I consider 'griot' to be my title. For me, that word combines the meanings of both 'activist' and 'actor.'"

We talked at length about the challenges of *playing* the role of an activist who works for justice for Black people in America—and then, when she's off set, actually *being* an activist working for the same. Given this, I couldn't help but ask if she had a clear mission for her work and her life. She, like Jordan, answered immediately.

"My focus is absolutely on collective liberation," she said. "To me, collective liberation means that every human being is able to live fully, safely in their fullest authenticity. And right now, that work really starts with Black liberation. As an actor, I feel like I'm a vessel that is seen and heard. But I also suspect that at some point, some of my work will also be in writing or creating meaningful experiences that also focus on that collective liberation."

Zuri's ability to clearly express her own ethic for her work and her advocacy is a trait several of the most successful and prolific activists I spoke to share. In fact, I wrote my own mission—my spark statement—several years ago, to clarify and codify what I wanted my life to stand for. Despite my adolescent disdain for my father's mission statement idea so long ago, I knew I needed a statement that could guide any decisions that I made going forward—from parenting to advocacy to everything in between.

I'll admit: articulating my personal mission took some time. In fact, I was prompted to do so only after I received an email from the ONE Campaign prior to the Kenya trip, asking me about the purpose behind the activism inherent in my work: my photographs, my blog, and books that I had authored or coauthored. I stared at the email for a moment, realizing that I didn't have any idea what to say, in any coherent manner. Because the question required a written response, I had to actually sit and think about the question: Why was I moved to create the work that I did?

Thinking back, it occurred to me that years earlier, perhaps around the time that I became a mother, I had become seriously disenchanted with media in general. I harbored no illusions about the fact that bad things happen in the world—events about which the media certainly has the responsibility to inform us. Yet I couldn't help but feel that news organizations, media conglomerates, and even individual journalists were starting to *relish* the communication of negativity and ugliness. Crime and gore and wrongdoing, and even sickness and sadness and desperation: these were quickly becoming *entertainment*. Magazines and billboards seemed to delight in screaming what was wrong with us and what we needed to do to "fix our flaws." Reality television exposing ugly sides of life was becoming commonplace.

And readers and viewers and buyers seemed to be lapping it all up.

This went against everything I knew to be true: I flat-out did not believe that the world was that bad. And so I set out to prove it. My book *The Beauty of Different* illustrated that people, in all their shapes and colors and sizes and genders and orientations and insights, are empirically, inarguably beautiful. I frequently shared photographs online of small, seemingly insignificant things to show; pictures that showed the goodness in the world, one image at a time. I began traveling as often as opportunity would allow, capturing images of beauty that were different from those that surrounded me at home, and I tried to share them as much as possible through social media. This practice—living into this belief in the beauty of the world—is what led to bigger and broader opportunities for activism, work that embodies the scope of everything I do today.

So, in the hope that it would help me answer that email from ONE, I decided to sit down and write a spark statement. By then, I'd been an avid journaler for some time, and I knew that I would be able to tap into an inner wisdom if I just stopped to listen to myself. I grabbed my journal and asked myself a few questions.

First, I thought, *What do I believe in?* In that moment, I wasn't thinking about my faith or religious beliefs as much as about my philosophies of life, parenting, leadership, and work. I asked myself what my duties are as a citizen of the planet. If I had been given these gifts in "trusteeship," as Mr. Arun Gandhi taught me, I wondered what I had been called to use them for. I thought about my strident belief that the world is inherently good and beautiful. I wrote down whatever came to mind, whether it seemed big or small. It felt good to simply get the ideas on paper, all in one place.

Then, after I'd exhausted that list, I asked myself, *If I had a magic wand, how would I change the world?* This may seem like a silly exercise, but really, why wouldn't I consider it? If, as Mr. Gandhi suggested, I'd been given skills and gifts that could make the world better, then why not consider the biggest and boldest changes I would make if I could? I journaled my biggest and wildest dreams for the world, and I detailed what it would look like if my dreams came true. I wrote down these things as if I actually *did* have the power to make them happen.

And then, armed with my answers to these two questions, as well as the list of things that I loved doing—that list of light words I'd made when I first decided to leave law—and I started to play with my spark statement. I wrote it in present tense: claiming that the things that I loved to do could help transform the world for the better. I wrote, and then took a break, and then returned to it, editing and massaging it some more. In the end, I came up with a statement that fully expresses the light I hoped to create with my work and my activism:

I believe in the interconnectedness of all who inhabit our planet.

I engage in the relentless pursuit of real, uncontrived beauty, in every form.

I illustrate that beauty is everywhere, even (and sometimes especially) in the most unlikely places.

In so doing, I work tirelessly to counter negativity, violence, discrimination, and desperation, and join forces with those who celebrate positivity, peace, kindness, and joy.

I convince the skeptical of their uncommon beauty, and I create tools to help the weary see the inherent power they hold in their own lives.

I provide hard, irrefutable evidence that there is good in the world, and I am fiercely dedicated to showing how beautiful our planet really is, one image at a time.

Armed with my new spark statement, I was able to respond to that email from ONE with confidence. Then, in a fit of courage, I decided to publish this spark statement on my blog as a way to truly hold myself accountable. It has been invaluable in helping me stay on purpose in my work in activism, and I use it as my North Star to this day. In "The Lightmaker's Manual" toward the back of this book, I share a more detailed process to help create your own spark statement. And once you've written your spark statement, you'll find it a treasured tool in keeping you true to your own values and mission.

◆ ◆ ◆

Activist and filmmaker Brad Montague is particularly fond of writing down and revisiting his personal mission as a way to codify his ethic. When I met with him, the world was several months into the COVID-19 pandemic, throwing plans many of us had for the foreseeable future out the window. In addition, the news in the United States was being dominated by stories of extreme bigotry and cruelty, resulting in civil unrest. So when I asked Brad about the mission of his activism going forward, his brow furrowed.

"I'll be honest with you, Karen," he began. "Right now, I'm in a foggy place of sorts, which has a lot to do with the pandemic, and the world at large. I thought I was going one way, but now, I'm not sure what I want next. And so my process going forward is to rewrite my manifesto."

"You have a manifesto?" This sounded suspiciously like a spark statement, so naturally, I was curious. "Tell me more."

He laughed. "Well in my opinion, more non-evil people l should write manifestos! I wrote my manifesto a while ago, and over time I've added to it. Sometimes I'll even rewrite it in different versions: I've written it as an actual manifesto, but sometimes I'll rewrite it as a prayer. Revisiting my manifesto helps me get greater clarity on what I believe, what I want, what is lacking in my life and my relationships, and what I want to add."

He took a deep breath. "It's really important to me to occasionally take the time to revisit my manifesto, so that I can pull back completely and focus on putting into words some of the beliefs I have that are nonnegotiable. It helps me to reaffirm the things that I have no questions about, that are true to who I am. The process of revisiting it helps me unlock all the next steps."

I love that Brad's manifesto is a living document. His explanation for spending time revisiting his manifesto reminded me, strangely, of a day about four years ago when I watched my daughter, Alexis, restring her guitar. Even though she had been playing guitar for almost two years and her guitar needed to be restrung every two months or so, I'd never actually seen her do it. The first few times the guitar had needed restringing, she'd taken it to a guitar store to have it done. Other times, she would have her guitar instructor help her during a lesson, usually when I was in another room.

"You know how to do that?" I asked in wonder, as she pulled packets of strings out of her guitar case.

"Of *course*, Mom," she said, barely suppressing an eye roll. "Every guitar player knows how to do this. Or they *should*."

So I watched. I noted how she unwound the old string and gently pulled it out, then equally carefully fed the new string into her guitar, winding it back on the tuners. A couple times she wound the string too tightly and it snapped. But Alex is nothing if not patient, and she simply worked the broken string back out of the guitar and replaced it with a spare. Then she tuned each string, used a wire cutter to trim the ends, and voilà: good as new. The process took longer than I would have thought, but she was meticulous about it. Alexis tells me that over time, strings build up oil and grime, so the sound of the instrument is totally different when it has new strings, and the guitar feels better to play.

Revisiting your spark statement can feel a bit like restringing a guitar. First you notice that something is off—that something about the mission you've created for your life and your advocacy a few years ago doesn't seem quite right anymore. So you meticulously revisit the words you wrote. Like Alex and her guitar, the process can be a bit laborious. Plans suddenly "snap"—you realize that some aspect of how you'd like your activism to play out has shifted or changed, or new circumstances in your life have come into play—and it has to be reworked and fixed. Things have to be tuned. And the trick is not to get wound too tightly while you're going through it all.

I've had my spark statement for more than a decade now, and I've referred to it many times over the years, making tweaks as necessary (although it's surprising how little I've had to adjust it over time). The longer I've had it, the more I love it—mostly because it is broad enough to encompass all the various iterations of the work I've done during those years. My spark statement kept me focused as I wrote my first book and continued to do so as I wrote this one. It has helped me hone my focus for my coaching career and most certainly for my own activism. This spark statement, in all of its iterations, has been a powerful guide when making big decisions about my life. Whatever lies ahead, I know I'll continue to refer to it to keep me headed toward my true north.

Because it reflects what I want my legacy to be.

7 | ON MIND MAPS, STAR CHARTS, AND TAKING FIRST STEPS

My friend Aimee Woodall has a heart as big as Texas. Aimee is the founder of the Giving Hub, the impressive distribution center established in Houston days after Hurricane Harvey made landfall. But the Giving Hub was only part of her activism around the storm. The rest of the story is more personal.

About four days after we evacuated our flooded home and were camping out at the house of our daughter's best friend's family, it began to dawn on us that our house was completely destroyed. The floodwaters hadn't yet receded, so we needed to figure out a place to live for the near future. My parents had evacuated their own home as a precaution, so staying with them was out. By this point, all the hotels and short-term-lease apartments in town were occupied by other displaced families. The family to whose home we'd evacuated— our daughter's friend's family—generously offered their space to us for as long as we needed it. We appreciated this sincere gesture, but I already felt like we were imposing on them. At the time, we barely knew them, save for the occasional sleepovers our daughters enjoyed. (Needless to say, they're now close friends of ours.) I wanted to give them back their privacy, and I was getting anxious about next moves.

That's when my cellphone rang. Aimee is one of those friends I go without seeing in person for long stretches. Then when we finally get together, it's usually at an hours-long meal.

"Where *are* you?!" she asked as soon as I answered the phone. She had been following our flood saga on Facebook, and her voice was filled with concern. "Are you okay?"

"We're fine. We're at the home of some friends while we figure out what we're going to do."

"Do you have a place to stay?"

"Well, not really . . ."

"Karen, I have a two-bedroom garage apartment that is sitting empty. You're going to stay with us, for as long as you need."

I stammered a bit, but she insisted. "Look," she said. Her voice was firm. "Either you're going to take it, or I'm going to offer it to some of the volunteers who have driven in from out of town to help." That's when she told me about the Giving Hub. "Honestly, I'll totally offer it to these volunteers, but I'd feel better if you took it because I already know you and your family. So you'd kind of be doing me a favor."

Well, when she put it like *that*. . . .

We gratefully took her up on her offer, and for about six weeks we made our home in her bright, airy apartment. It was the perfect place to regroup as we looked for a more permanent living situation. I'm not sure how we'll ever repay Aimee and her family's kindness, but we're going to die trying.

A couple of months after we moved into a place of our own, I reached out to Aimee to catch up and insist that I at least buy her dinner and drinks—my feeble attempt at beginning to pay down that debt. We met at a local bistro and, as usual, lost track of time reconnecting. That evening, our conversation reminded me that generosity and advocacy have always been a part of who Aimee is. But she also reminded me of another lesson I've since taken to heart: the world doesn't need to see you make your initial moves into advocacy. In Aimee's case, sometimes her work has been behind-the-scenes stealthy.

You see, in addition to starting the Giving Hub, Aimee is also the founder of a branding firm here in Houston that works solely with organizations who have a focus on giving back to their communities: both nonprofits and for-profit companies with a strong sustainability ethic as part of their core values. While her agency has been around for many years, a few years earlier she had sent out an email announcing that, going forward, she would only be working with organizations committed to sustainability and social justice. I thought it was both the bravest and the riskiest thing I'd ever seen. So that evening, as we caught up over our dinner and drinks, I brought it up.

"I still can't believe you did it," I said, taking a sip of my cocktail. "I mean, I love that you did, but I was really worried you'd go out of business by excluding organizations that didn't do any sustainable work. And yet you've grown your business by multiples and you're thriving. How the hell did you know?"

"I *didn't* know," she smiled. "All I knew was that I wanted our work to be about making the world better."

I wasn't satisfied. "I mean, that's cool and all," I pressed. "But how did you know you would end up surviving? It was such a huge risk!"

"Well," she answered slowly. "It actually *wasn't* a big risk. Again, I just knew that I wanted my work to be meaningful, and to do that, I had to make sure my clients were also doing meaningful work."

I stared at her, still confused. "But *how?* How did you make that happen? And how did you know that once you culled those who weren't interested in giving back to the community that there would be enough clients left that you'd still be able to make a living? Did you audit your clients? I bet that went over like a lead balloon."

"Not exactly," she laughed. "Okay, so here's the truth: by the time I announced to the world what we were going to be about, we were already working that way. We'd completed the contracts for most of our other clients, and over time, we had gradually begun to only choose clients who were committed to putting good in the world. By the time that announcement went out, all but two of our clients at the time were either nonprofits or had strong sustainability initiatives in-house."

"Ooooh," I said. "So you already had *evidence* that it was going to be a success, even before you told everyone!"

"Absolutely. We'd been taking baby steps in that direction for a couple of years. By the time it was announced, we were already there."

I sat back, impressed. The expression "real Gs move in silence" immediately came to mind. In essence, it means that pros don't crow about something amazing that they're doing before it happens or while it's happening; instead, they just quietly focus on making it happen, knowing that in time, the work will speak for itself. It occurred to me that this phrase captured Aimee's philosophy: when she saw a situation where her gifts and talents could be used to serve, she just quietly got to work. Like when she shifted the focus of her business. Or cofounded a food distribution center, which would grow big enough to garner the attention of a former president, in the middle of a hurricane.

Or quietly offered her garage apartment to a friend in need.

Aimee's decision to move in silence as she shifted her clientele focus before making an announcement made good business sense.

Now, years later, it occurs to me that this wisdom could be used in any new venture, including and especially when we intend to engage in more activism and advocacy. When we realize that we have gifts that could be used to help the world, it can be a very vulnerable space: What if people think my idea is dumb? What if people tell me I'm wasting my time? What if it doesn't even work?

In this era of broadcasting everything on social media—from who we're hanging out with to the foam art in our lattes—we often forget that we don't have to tell anyone what we're doing, at least in the moment we're doing it. We can take baby steps toward our brilliant ideas. We can beta-test concepts with friends. We can try out the waters before we wade in. And most importantly, we can quietly listen to leaders in our activism spaces: folks who have been doing this work long before we entered, and who are members of communities who are affected by our activism. We do this to learn of our own roles in the oppression they might be facing, the ways we can truly be of service, and how to avoid inadvertently causing harm.

Then, when we announce our dive into the deep end, we can do so with confidence, because we already know we know how to swim.

◆ ◆ ◆

The question of how to take those first few vulnerable steps, even if you're planning to quietly do so, is one I still wrestle with as my own advocacy grows and evolves. By now you know how much I love writing in my well-worn journal. And you've probably figured out that as much as I love free-spirited expression, I also love a process. And a planner. And a map. I love logic, and a well-thought-out flowchart makes my soul sing. (You can take the girl out of engineering, but it appears you can't take the engineering out of the girl.)

And so, for all my journal-writing and spark-statement-making, answering the question of what first steps I need to take when entering into a new aspect of advocacy requires tapping into my analytical brain. I'm continually charting out, in a concrete way, what my work and activism will look like, especially if I hope to do work and advocacy that fills me with meaning, purpose, and joy.

Over years of coaching my own clients, as well as much experimentation, I came up with two tools that help you process your goals and intentions, diagramming everything from where you stand in the present moment to where you'd like to go in the future. One of them is a mind map, and the other I call a star chart. Unlike a spark statement, which tends to remain unaltered for long periods of time, you will want to revisit your mind map and star chart regularly—not only to keep you purposeful about staying on track, but also to unearth other potential paths to your values and intentions.

First, a mind map is a visual way to brainstorm ideas—Wikipedia calls it "a diagram used to represent words, ideas, tasks, or other items linked to and arranged around a central key word or idea." Most of us don't think in a linear fashion, and a mind map offers a way to visually capture all the thoughts that ignite and spark while we're trying to work something out. To create a mind map, you start with a main concept in the middle and draw outward; as with most brainstorming activities, the trick is to make sure you don't censor yourself as you write. A mind map can help you get everything down on paper first; once you've exhausted all your ideas, then you can start evaluating what you've written.

Second, once you've brainstormed all the possible avenues you could take, pick your favorite and create a star chart. A star chart is, essentially, a goal map: a way to chart out the milestones toward your goal. But it's more than that: it's a mindful way to not only clarify your goal but also dig into why the goal is important to you. Star charts help you align your goal with your values and your spark statement; they provide a way to itemize the skills, education, and experience that you already have and that you take on your journey. I've used this tool to help clients clarify their personal goals, and they've said it's the best goalsetting framework they've ever used.

Here's an example: say you're hoping to tackle food insecurity in your community, and your light words are *gardening, songwriting*, and *performing*. If you're not sure how to begin, you'd grab your journal and on a blank page, you might brainstorm, using a mind map. First you'd write *food insecurity* in the middle of the page, with *gardening, songwriting*, and *performing* written around it. This could prompt some ideas that you'd write in the spaces around the words, by asking yourself questions like: How could you use gardening to help fight food insecurity? You'd jot your ideas down as fast as they came to you: *create a workshop teaching people to garden. Begin a community garden in a vacant lot. Start a food pantry with other gardeners in the area.* You would brainstorm all the different ways that gardening could help fight food insecurity, without censoring yourself in any way. Next, you'd move on to songwriting: How could you use songwriting to fight food insecurity? Again you'd brainstorm, exhausting all your ideas. Then you'd do the same with performing.

Once you've brainstormed all your ideas, you'd take a look at each of them to determine which feels like it would be the most fun to do. These become the goals around which you'd build a star chart on another clean page of your journal (or poster, or whiteboard), plotting the steps it would take to achieve that goal, and ensuring that as you take those steps, you're harnessing all your prior experience, your mission, and your vision for how it will look when you've achieved your goal.

I strongly recommend mind maps and star charts as tools that clarify your way forward, no matter whether you're already a seasoned advocate or just beginning your activist journey. The process for creating each of them is simple. (See "The Lightmaker's Manual" toward the back of this book for creating your own mind map and star chart.)

Entering into activism or advocacy work can feel terrifying, but remember: you can go at your own pace. Take the time to think about what your mission is, what your star statement would look like, what you want your legacy to be. And then brainstorm. What are all the ways you could live into your spark statement? What could you try? What would the steps look like on your way to making this happen? Take some time to sit and think through this. Then, armed with your star chart, get ready to quietly take steps in that direction.

Just like a real G would.

In the aftermath of Hurricane Harvey, my husband and I walked around what remained of our house, stunned. After two weeks of dank, filthy water taking up residence in our home, half of our furniture had literally exploded from the moisture. We had lost everything. Anything that was two feet or below in our house was obliterated, and most things above twenty-five inches had to be discarded—especially if they were made of cloth or paper, because all our research had indicated that mold ain't no joke. So all clothes, books, and papers—with the exception of what we had evacuated with—were gone. We packed up all the items we could save—

one or two pieces of furniture we'd managed to elevate before we evacuated, dishes stored in upper cabinets, that sort of thing—and placed them in a storage pod about ten miles away. Removing the drywall revealed studs so rotten that many no longer reached the floor (convincing me that pure magic was keeping the house from completely caving in). The dining room had actually begun *sinking*. And of course everything smelled.

"What are we going to do?" I said, looking around helplessly.

"Well, we could sell." Marcus is always a pragmatist. "I mean, we bought this house below current land value. We could cut our losses and move somewhere else."

"I don't want to sell," I suddenly responded. "I mean, I don't know if we can afford to stay here, but I think we should try." I turned to look Marcus in the eye. "I think our goal should be to make Hurricane Harvey be, in hindsight, *one of the most meaningful things that has happened to us, ever.*"

It was a crazy thought then, and years later, it still seems crazy. But the truth is that no matter what we did, we were starting from the very beginning. Harvey had given us a clean slate. There was nothing to do but embrace it and see what we could create going forward. As the saying goes: every new beginning comes from some beginning's end.

My friend Stephanie Wittels Wachs actually *lives* this saying. Stephanie and I met about a year after Harvey, at a fundraiser for a local charity. She was pregnant with her second child, a son, and she practically shimmered with life; she was warm, funny, and we immediately clicked. At that luncheon, I learned Stephanie is the author of a brilliant book, *Everything Is Horrible and Wonderful*, and that despite her quick laughter, she had faced true hardship in her own life. A few years earlier, her brother—actor, comic, and writer

SPARK

Harris Wittels—lost his fight against heroin addiction. During that same time, Stephanie's daughter was born with bilateral deafness.

Nevertheless, the grief from both of these events ended up prompting Stephanie to do some beautiful things. She created a scholarship fund in her brother's name for aspiring artists graduating from his alma mater, and she fiercely fought for a bill in the Texas state legislature that would compel insurance companies to cover hearing aids for deaf babies, since the devices were inexplicably considered "cosmetic." The bill passed.

A few months after the fundraiser, Stephanie and I reconnected, and we talked about the overarching feeling of terror we both felt in the wake of the events that changed us: a hurricane, her brother's death, her baby's deafness. We decided that perhaps the way to get through difficulty is not to find your way *out* but to find your way *up*. "There's a survival instinct that can happen when you start to freak out about things," she said. "At some point you just have to put it in perspective, because you don't have the capacity to worry and fret over *all* of it. It's too much. So instead, focus on the thing that totally matters, and then you see what you can make of it."

Whether your activism begins with a bang or a whisper, stepping out into the world of activism for the first time can be terrifying. Stephanie's activism began with a bang. The tragic death of her brother, combined with the discovery that her newborn baby girl was deaf, launched her quickly into change-making. But even if you've engaged in tons of introspection and have created a fully detailed mind map and star chart to lead the way, coming up with an idea to change the world is a scary thing to do. Of course, you've got to try anyway. The upside is just too great.

The thing is, if fear or anxiety is keeping you from taking those first steps, "try anyway" can feel like pretty useless advice. Fear can be pretty paralyzing. But even when the very first step feels too great, it can be helpful to think of what one *tiny* step you can take in the direction of progress toward that first milestone.

Sometimes a tiny step is all it takes.

◆ ◆ ◆

Jane Mosbacher Morris is the founder and chief executive officer of TO THE MARKET, a socially inspired enterprise aimed at economic empowerment of women around the world. Through the sourcing and manufacturing of apparel, accessories, and home goods in a socially and economically responsible manner, and by providing full transparency within the retail supply chain, Jane and her team work with huge brands and retailers to provide what she calls "story-rich" products, all while ensuring that the creators of those products enjoy meaningful work and get paid what their work is worth.

I met Jane at a conference hosted by the ONE Campaign to educate journalists and bloggers about the ways poverty dispro-portionately affects women. From the lack of electricity that makes it dangerous for women when they give birth, to the difficulty of keeping girls in schools to get an education when their incomes are needed for their families' survival, to other grim issues like slav-ery and sex trafficking: the toll of poverty on women and girls is immense. During breaks we met with each other and with confer-ence speakers—physicians and activists and politicians and authors and actors—to discuss what we had heard. It was during one of these breaks that I was introduced to Jane, a congenial young woman with impossibly kind eyes. But I quickly learned that behind those eyes was the soul of an unmitigated badass.

I loved Jane immediately, so I was happy that we continued to run into each other over the years. I slowly learned bits and pieces of her impressive background, one that has nothing to do with retail or fashion. For most of her working life, her expertise was in—improbably enough—counterterrorism. I was curious how a counterterrorism operative ends up as a retail executive helping to lift women out of poverty, but luckily for me, Jane is incredibly open about her journey to her call to activism and how she made the leap from one career to the next. I soon learned that she'd executed her advocacy plan through a series of baby steps—steps toward a destination that, in hindsight, her entire life had prepared her for.

Jane was in high school when the September 11 terrorist attacks on the World Trade Center and Pentagon occurred, and the experience inspired her to pursue a degree in global politics. She was accepted to Georgetown University, and while a student there, she scored an internship with the US Department of State working in counterterrorism. Even before she graduated, she had moved from a part-time internship to full-time employment. While still a student, she created leadership training programs with women in Afghanistan by working with local nongovernmental organizations and Afghanistan's Ministry of Interior Affairs.

"I was one of the only women in the office," she remembers:

And I also learned that in our efforts to counter terror we, as a government, weren't engaging women. We were largely engaging faith leaders, believing that they were responsible for the radicalization of young kids. But I know that we women around the world are the primary conveyor of norms. I knew that while you might have someone in your faith tradition communicating violence, it is the parents, primarily mothers, who teach children what's okay and what's not okay. And the way you engage women, especially in societies where they are disenfranchised and have no political or financial voice, is that you help them.

"This is so interesting," I responded, taking in her words. "I mean, it makes sense that empowering women is good for the world: poverty disproportionately affects women, and helping a woman gain financial independence improves the economic wellness of her entire community. But I hadn't considered the effect it might have on national and international security."

"Right," Jane smiled as she continued. "So much of the security work I was doing was about creating economic stability in a country; specifically, exploring how to give women the opportunity to earn, inherit, or share the money of the local economy, so that they have influence in their communities. At first, people didn't understand what I was trying to do, but eventually, I gained support for my programs. And as a result, I definitely began to feel deeply connected to the ability of women to chart their own destiny."

After Jane graduated, she continued to work at the State Department, eventually pursuing an MBA at Columbia University. While there, she moved into a new position working with then–Secretary of State Hillary Clinton on global women's issues. In this job, Jane had a broader portfolio called "Women, Peace & Security," which included not only counterterrorism but also human trafficking, sexual assault, and domestic violence. "So my work wasn't just about women and terrorism in the security sector anymore but also more pointedly focused on creating opportunities for women," Jane says. "This experience just further imprinted on me my need to focus on women's rights."

After graduating from Columbia, Jane eventually left the State Department and was hired to work at the McCain Institute by

Cindy McCain, widow of the late US senator John McCain. "They needed someone to oversee their humanitarian action, which is mostly focused on human trafficking," Jane remembered:

Both at the State Department, and the McCain Institute, I'd learned that retail manufacturing, which includes traditional factory work but also artisan work, is the second largest economy in the developing world. And this industry is dominated by women. But while they *are* the majority of makers, whether as artisans or working in the production line in an old-school factory, they *aren't* the majority of the people in the industry actually earning the big money. On the other hand, agriculture, which is the largest economy, already had a lot of sophisticated and meaningful investment. The retail space had the most opportunity for improvement. Being a part of the McCain Institute was how I became really aware of the extent to which there is labor exploitation and trafficking in the retail industry.

By now, Jane was finally able to articulate and name her personal mission—her spark statement. "After all those years, it became clear to me that my personal call was about creating dignity of work, opportunity, and choice for women," Jane said. "And I truly believed that retail could be the way I could do it." Her idea to create TO THE MARKET was born.

"Was retail something that you'd always been interested in?" I asked.

She laughed, louder than I would have expected. "Oh no," she grinned. "If you had told me while I was working on counterterrorism that I would end up working in retail, I would've looked at you in *total* disbelief. Honestly, I think I would have even said retail is a vapid industry. Besides, I had *no* retail experience. In fact, I remember when I first started TO THE MARKET, someone asked me what experience I had in retail. The only thing that popped into my head was that I was named 'Best Dressed' my sophomore year of high school!"

What's so interesting about Jane's story is that she had an idea for how she could change the world, but in a space—retail—in which she had no experience (although admittedly, she had a lot of related knowledge that she could bring to bear). This mirrors how most people enter into activism: they are ignited by a problem that needs to be addressed, but doing so requires them to take action that they have never taken before and that might even be in an arena that's foreign to them. So I asked Jane: if someone is interested in moving into advocacy, especially when they might feel ill-equipped, what is her best advice? How do they take that first step?

Jane thought for a moment. "Well," she began slowly, "I think it's very easy to get into what I call a despair spiral, or analysis paralysis, when trying to figure out how to tackle a problem. So I think my answer is the same, whether the question is about activism or any other challenge: I focus on the three circles that I'm in the middle of, concentric circles that surround me. The first, smallest circle represents what I can *control*. The second, larger circle that encloses the first circle is what I can *influence*. Then the third, largest circle is everything else. So for me, focusing first on what I can control and influence is a helpful mindset."

There's a great word that emerges from Zen Buddhism: *shoshin*, which means "beginner's mind." It's related to Jane's advice of focusing first on what you can control and influence, and then going from there. The *shoshin* concept means approaching an issue with the openness and zeal for learning that a beginner does, even when the issue is something that you think you already know everything about. Not only does a beginner's mind help you unearth perspectives and data to which you might have otherwise been blind; you might even have some fun along the way. Furthermore, remaining in a beginner's mind helps to minimize the possibility that you will run roughshod over those who are already a part of the activism community, particularly if you're in a privileged demographic. Being a continual learner is never a bad strategy, especially when helping a community of which you're not a member, and you might potentially and unintentionally cause more harm than good.

In other words, look at where you want to go, and then cultivate a mindset that's open to learning and experimenting with the steps on your way there.

This is the advice of my friend Tarana Burke. Tarana is the brilliant activist who began the Me Too movement, a revolution of support, resources, and healing for survivors of sexual violence. Tarana's amazing advocacy has garnered numerous accolades, including being named the 2017 *Time* magazine Person of the Year and receiving the 2018 Courage Prize from the Ridenhour Prizes, awarded to individuals who "demonstrate courageous defense of the public interest and passionate commitment to social justice."

Tarana was a tireless activist for decades prior to 2017, when actress Alyssa Milano popularized the #MeToo hashtag on Twitter in response to the sexual abuse allegations against film producer Harvey Weinstein. Milano's tweet brought Tarana's work to national attention. Tarana has been an activist since 1989, working in defense and service of sexual abuse survivors. Tarana and I have known each other for several years, and she is a person of both fierce determination and joy. So naturally she was one of the first people I asked for advice on how to get started in activism.

Her immediate answer reinforced the importance of a continuous learner's mindset. "I advise young people—or really anyone wanting to be more involved in reshaping the world—to do a few things first. The first is to get clear about who they are," she explained. "For instance, when I first started out, I got really clear that I was a 'worker,' and my role was to roll up my sleeves and help advance the work I believed in with my skills behind the scenes. That clarity helped me not feel jealous for not being able to contribute in the ways *other* people had deemed valuable."

"This process of getting clear and doing self-assessment can take time," she continued. "Folks often feel pressured to know and understand their role immediately and do tangible or visible things right away. For this reason, the other, equally important thing I advise is to get out in the world and develop a better understanding of the issue you care about. Volunteer, attend meetings, join groups, and allow yourself to be open to deepening your education." Tarana's mindful approach also allows her to learn what she needs to know so that she can engage in her activism thoughtfully, minimizing the chances of her inadvertently causing harm to the communities for which she advocates.

Mira Jacob, the author of *Good Talk* and an antiracism and LGBTQ+ activist, concurs. Going slowly into activism and having a beginner's mind are crucial. Mira is also adamant about the huge benefit that curiosity brings to beginning a path to activism.

"I think of curiosity as the immigrant's superpower," Mira grinned. "The cool thing about my parents—and I mean *deeply* cool—is that as immigrants, they were always trying to figure out America. When they came here in their twenties, they knew almost nothing about the country. They ran into people who wanted to know all about them and people who wanted them to leave, and they made a lot of mistakes on their way to figuring out how to live here."

Even years later, Mira said, after their lives were fully established in New Mexico, they never stopped trying to figure out America. And they did it with enthusiasm. And bewilderment, and excitement, and *always* in the spirit of curiosity. "Because of them, curiosity is at the core of all of the work I do," Mira told me. "Curiosity, I think, is the antidote to so much of the fear and hatred we see around us."

So there you have it: be clear on your scope of control and influence, approach your issue with a beginner's mind, and maintain a sense of curiosity. This is all great advice for how to take those very first steps on your activism journey. But I'd like to add one more thing: When it comes to that very first baby step, *dare yourself.*

I'm not generally a daring person. You'll never see me tie a bungee cord around my ankle and take a flying leap off of a perfectly good bridge. Airplanes are things that I try assiduously to remain inside of while flying, as opposed to leaping out of them with a parachute strapped to my back. If life or limb is on the line, I'm going to walk away. Yet I admit that some of the biggest things I've experienced occurred because I dared myself. I just sort of quietly said, "Huh. Let's see if I can."

As a young engineer, only about one year out of university, I could already see that engineering was not a career I wanted to pursue long-term. I was working for an engineering construction company, and day in and day out I spent hours calculating what steel beams and girders and columns would make the best pipe racks. When I looked over the cubicle wall at the engineer sitting next to me—the guy with twenty years more experience than I had—I saw that he was doing the same thing, just with bigger, more complicated pipe racks.

So I began toying with the idea of going back to university for a graduate degree. At the time, the only reasonable options I thought I had was to pursue an MBA or a law degree. Many engineers I knew were getting their MBAs. So just to be different, I decided to consider law.

In all honesty, going to law school seemed like a pipe dream. My undergraduate grades were average, and I assumed that only the very best and brightest would get into law school. That group certainly didn't include me. Why even try? I thought to myself. But my inner daredevil answered: I dare you to look into it.

So I did. In addition to my undergraduate transcripts, applying to law school would require that I take the LSAT. One day after work I stopped at a bookstore to thumb through an LSAT preparation book, to see what types of questions the entrance exam would contain. I wanted to see what it would be like in case I actually broke down and decided to try.

This doesn't look impossible, I thought, surprised, as I flipped the pages.

I dare you to take the LSAT, my daredevil responded. *No one has to see how you do. And you don't actually have to apply to law school. You've got nothing to lose. Take it and see what happens.*

So I bought the prep book, took it home, studied, and applied to take the LSAT the next time it was offered. When I received my scores, I was shocked: I had done well. *Really* well.

Maybe I *should* apply to law school! I thought.

And again, my daredevil piped up. *I dare you to. What's the worst that can happen? You won't get in? So what? You have a job; you don't actually need a law degree. I dare you to try.*

And so I did. I applied to two major law schools in Houston and received acceptance letters from both. And so . . . I had to go. After all, how could I turn back now?

What seemed to me as an insurmountable dream of becoming a lawyer happened because I dared myself to take baby steps along the way. Other major events have happened in my life because of baby steps. I became a scuba diver because I dared myself to check out a class. I took that photo assignment to Kenya because I dared myself to say yes to the invitation from the ONE Campaign. Heck, I even became a mother because I dared myself to contact an adoption agency just to see what the process was all about.

So as you go into the world of advocacy, dare yourself. Dare yourself to learn more about the issues. Dare yourself to examine what's in your control and who you can influence. Dare yourself to take that first step. The best thing that will happen is that you'll actually change the world.

8 | ON LISTENING, INTENTIONS, AND DOING IT FOR FUN'S SAKE

A few years ago, I had a dinner with a friend I hadn't seen in more than a decade. Terra is a lawyer and a former coworker, and although we didn't work together very long, we immediately clicked. After I left my job, we mostly lost touch, save for her occasional emails sharing an interesting quote or food for thought. I don't remember how we reconnected, but when we did, after a quick email exchange, we decided to schedule an early dinner to catch up. As we should have expected, our dinner went late into the evening. Terra is one of those people with whom you quickly find yourself having deep conversations, and you leave your time together thinking about things differently.

Our conversation meandered all evening long, until at one point we turned to the topic of goal-setting. "I read this interesting article about how to achieve goals without becoming obsessive," she mentioned as she sipped her wine.

"Really?" I was intrigued, having a bit of an obsessive streak of my own. "How?"

"Well, first," she leaned forward, almost conspiratorially, "You think of a goal. *Then*, you think of the associated ritual that would help you achieve it. So for example: if your goal is to lose twenty pounds, then the ritual could be a commitment to eat healthily and move every day."

I raised an eyebrow. "That's it? This doesn't seem revolutionary. Isn't this what we normally do?"

"Ah, but here's the key," she said. "Once you've figured out the ritual, you focus on *that* instead of on the goal. So you try to forget about the twenty pounds and instead focus on doing the ritual. At the end of each day, you evaluate: Did I move today? Did I eat healthily? And if you did, great, mission accomplished. If you didn't, you don't worry about it and you try again the following day. The result, this article said, is that you'll end up achieving your true goal—to be fitter and healthier—and the bonus is that you'll probably meet or even exceed your original goal or decide that the original goal wasn't that important. Either way, you'll discover that the ritual itself was really the important thing in the first place."

Huh. *Forget the goal; focus on the ritual.* It's an intriguing approach, and I could see how this might work with small things—for example, my journaling practice. When I first began journaling, my original *goal* was to fill a journal a month. My *ritual* was to create something—anything—in my journal at least once a day, at least five days per week. Of course, occasionally I'd skip a day but today, as I look at my bookshelf, I see more than a dozen completed journals, and that doesn't count the several dozen that were casualties of Hurricane Harvey. Quite by accident and purely by ritual, I'm a prolific diarist; it turns out this is more important to me than my initial intention to churn out a journal a month. I've even become quite good at it. But how could this ritual theory apply to activism?

Terra's words came rushing back to me after my conversation with activist and faith leader Valarie Kaur. It's her counsel that practice is exactly how we should approach our activism. "The labor for justice is going to continue on after we die," Valarie to me, "and it was happening before we were born. So the truth is, we may not ever see the fruits of our labor. We have to learn how to make the labor *an end in itself*."

Well, that's depressing, isn't it? As activists, we might never see the end of our work. We may never witness the end of discrimination, injustice, or environmental crisis. But we can keep going by focusing on the process: the practices that enable us to make forward progress toward the ultimate goal. And we can celebrate the moments of joy that such practices and rituals can bring. Valarie continued, "We *must* labor with joy. It is the only way to find longevity in the labor." Otherwise, of course, we risk burnout.

The practices you employ may vary, depending on where your spark statement leads you. Your practices might involve journaling, in order to keep a record of your progress. Or your practice might be letter-writing. Or your practice might be honing your craft: those skills that Mr. Gandhi shared are given to us in trusteeship for service to the world. By tapping into your light words, the possibilities for practice are limitless: knitting blankets for premature babies in your local neonatal unit, for example. Running marathons to bring awareness to a social issue. With some thought, you can probably come up with countless actions to ritualize your advocacy work. When you do, your activism becomes a mindfulness practice in and of itself.

◆ ◆ ◆

Two practices in particular can ensure that you stay on track with your mission while also cultivating moments of joy. The first practice is listening.

An important aspect of my training to become a leadership coach was the concept of *mindful listening*. Mindful listening is, in essence, paying attention with a heaping side of empathy. The benefits of cultivating this practice are numerous: it leads to conversations that go deeper than surface-level chats, it enhances clarity and insight, and it offers an emotionally positive experience for both the listener and listened-to. And while this practice is essential in coaching and counseling, it's also helpful in advocacy. When you interact with a member of a community for whose cause you are hoping to help advocate, for example, you need to listen mindfully, to ensure you fully understand the issues they face and what role you might play. Or when you are talking with someone who holds an opposite view than you do, mindful listening can help you reach for deeper understanding.

One way to think about staying in mindful listening is to imagine *losing yourself in someone's story*. Here's what I mean: I can't tell you how many times I've seen *Star Wars: A New Hope (Episode IV)*—the one released in the 1970s, the first one in the Star Wars series in which we're introduced to Luke Skywalker, Han Solo, Princess Leia, and all the classic characters—but it's a lot. I saw it in a movie theater when I was a kid, many times in the years that followed, and since I'm married to a science fiction movie buff, several times a year during our decades-long marriage. I can practically recite the thing, is what I'm saying.

Still, each time I see the movie, I get completely lost in the story. I feel a thrill when Luke discovers that Old Ben Kenobi is actually

Obi-Wan Kenobi, the famed Jedi warrior. I'm terrified when Han, Leia, and Luke are almost killed by the giant garbage compactor on the Death Star. And I celebrate along with Luke and Han at the end, when they're receiving their royal commendations from the Princess. I feel these things *every time*. I am somehow able to put myself in Luke's shoes, even though at no point in my life have I ever been a young Tatooine farm boy. I empathize with his motivations and struggles, keeping any judgment about Luke's choices completely out of my mind. I'm not considering rebuttals to Luke's decisions, or how I would have made better ones as I watch; I'm simply immersing myself in the movie.

Mindful listening means getting lost in the speaker's story. When we're speaking to someone who might need our help or our advocacy, we can listen mindfully, paying attention to their story and reaching for empathy. When we're listening to someone honestly share their opinions, losing ourselves in their story can help us reach some level of understanding even if we disagree with their conclusions. Also, it bears noting that mindful listening is the primary way we stay in "beginner's mind": we set aside judgment, or any of the ways that we think we might "know better," especially as we learn from those who have labored longer than we have or who are members of a community who are letting us know what they need for their own liberation. The point is that getting into someone else's story might be the most effective tool we have in activism.

There are other practices for improving your listening. Asha Dornfest is a stellar listener: when you're in conversation with her, it feels like she is looking deep into your soul. Listening is a practice at which she's naturally gifted, but when I asked her what role listening plays in her activism, she assured me that anyone can do it.

"Anyone can cultivate intentional listening skills," she explained, "and it's important *especially* if you aspire to be an activist. It can be as simple as taking a beat when you hear something: increasing the time between when you hear something and when you react, so that the velocity of an interaction isn't so fast." This concept of slowing down the velocity of an interaction is a brilliant one. Taking a moment to think about and absorb what you're hearing, rather than rushing to judgment or even a witty retort, is a good way to remain in mindfulness.

My artist friend Jordan Seaberry takes a totally different but equally effective approach: he uses his artmaking as a practice for listening. When we met, he explained it to me: "I engage in a process that I call 'call-and-response,' and I use that phrase in the historical sense, in the way it arose during African American enslavement." He began,

It goes like this: when I have a blank canvas, at first I have no idea what's going on it. So I create a layer. Then that layer calls for something else. I respond by putting that element in, and then it calls for something else. Often I'll do the first layer, the first element, and then maybe a second element, and I'll think to myself, "Oh, it's great. It's done. It's perfect." Then I'll go to sleep, and in the morning I realize that the painting is actually calling for something else. When you look at my paintings, the surfaces are thick, they're messy, they're covered with paint and mixed media collage, so that in the end, the first layer is completely invisible. There are, in essence, finished paintings under every painting.

So for me, the meaning is made on the canvas itself. It's not that I have an idea, and then I translate it on canvas, which I think is how a lot of artists work. That's a fine way to make art, but it's just not how I do it. For me, I start with a clean slate, and the ideas and meanings are hashed out on the canvas itself, through what I call "the life of the painting." The way I see it, it's the same in organizing and activism: the meaning of the relationship with a person that you're working with grows and exists through the life of the relationship. It's iterative. I don't approach someone thinking, "Karen believes XYZ thing, and I need to convince her of these other things." It is a process wherein you give me a call, and let me know what you need, and I respond to that. And then we go back and forth. It's call-and-response. Relationships in activism are identical.

I was intrigued. "So your practice of listening in art—of call-and-response—is actually your practice of listening in activism?"

"Oh, absolutely!" Jordan was emphatic. "It's not just what I'm doing or what I'm trying to accomplish; it's about the stance in which I do it. It's about the process, the practice. Painting is its own process. Organizing is its own process. And one process informs the other."

I love this idea of a tangible, creative, joyful practice for improving listening. Both losing yourself in a speaker's story and slowing down the pace of a conversation will get you a long way toward developing true expertise in mindful listening; adding in a practice like painting could ensure you can really focus on the call-and-response. In truth, any meditative practice—sitting in stillness, taking silent walks, even knitting—can enhance your ability to mindfully listen. The lesson of Jordan's art is to find such a practice and truly make it your own.

The second practice, one that builds upon mindful listening, is tapping into your own inner wisdom. A daily mindfulness practice helps you stay within the values and mission dictated by your spark statement and also cultivate a sense of joy.

A few years ago, I stumbled upon an article that outlined an intention-setting practice by author and meditation teacher Mallika Chopra, whose work focuses on personal wellness. (Unfortunately I can't remember the title of the article or where it appeared.) But I found this daily practice so meaningful that I've started every day by meditating on these prompts. Sometimes I write them in my journal, and other times I use them as a form of meditation before getting out of bed. This practice consists of asking three questions.

The first question is, *What will make me feel connected today?* Answering this question allows you to look for an opportunity during the day to practice mindful listening—to lose yourself in another person's story. This prompt is about caring for important relationships, which might include personal relationships but can often include relationships with people related to the activism you've identified in your spark statement. Your answer to this prompt might involve something big, like scheduling a meeting with other activists to determine if you can join forces for a particular action. Sometimes it's something smaller, like sending an email of appreciation to a friend, colleague, or family member. Either way, this daily question prompts you to consider how to remain connected to those around you since, as Jordan says, so much of activism is about relationships.

The second question is, *What will make me feel healthy today?* This question leads to the practice of self-compassion, a huge part of activism; we'll discuss this later in this book. For now, this question is broad enough to allow you to answer freely, without constrictions, and tailor it to your needs of the day. One day it might make you feel healthy to hit the weights hard at the gym; another day, feeling healthy might look like a leisurely walk. On still another, you might want to show compassion for yourself by taking a media break from the bad news of the world so you can rest and recover. Or maybe you'll drink extra water. In any event, taking a moment to tune in and determine what you need for your own mental, physical, and emotional health is important. Self-care is necessary if, as Valarie Kaur says, we are to find longevity in the labor of activism.

The final question is, *What will give me a sense of purpose today?* This might be my favorite of the three questions, because it calls us to ask what we can do to serve others, bring ourselves and others joy, and make light. Perhaps on one day you need to engage in some purposeful, quiet activism—like the simple moves my friend Aimee Woodall makes to set herself up for bigger acts in the future. On another, it might be to extend a gesture of simple but radical kindness—a small act that measurably improves someone's day. Or maybe you'll simply donate to a cause that's important to you. The beauty of this question is that it allows you to stay on task with regard to your larger activist purpose but also gives you the flexibility to alter it from day to day.

In the end, approaching activism as a process rather than an end goal may, ironically, be the way we make real progress toward our purpose. It is certainly the way to create moments of joy and connection along the way. As I was writing this chapter, I reached out to my friend Terra and told her that I would be including her wisdom about focusing on the ritual rather than the goal in these pages. She immediately emailed back, thanking me and telling me she has continued to track the practices in her life, resulting in her feeling more peaceful, purposeful, and healthy than she ever has before.

She gave me permission to share her story and ended her email with a simple but profound thought: "It is in the living that we create a life, my kindred soul," she wrote. Indeed.

♦ ♦ ♦

About a year after that trip to Kenya, I returned to Africa with the ONE Campaign, this time to Ethiopia. As before, I traveled with a group of writers and bloggers, but my marching orders were different: instead of writing stories about what I witnessed for my own website, I was tasked with shadowing the others with my camera as they listened to the stories of medical and economic advances that were fighting poverty and preventable disease. My images of the trip were for my travel companions to use in their articles and blog posts, but of course I was free to use the photographs on my site as well.

I love writing, but photography *really* ignites my soul. As we saw earlier, the word *photography* means "drawing with light," and it is literally the way I approach my practice. I examine how light falls on my subject and figure out how to manipulate my camera and frame the shot to capture its beauty. The idea of doing that for eight to ten hours every day for a week was almost too joyful for me to contemplate.

And so off I went to meet my travel companions in Addis Ababa. Together we traveled all over the country learning about the art and culture, as well as the economic and technological innovations resulting from the creativity of local scientists, faith leaders, urban developers, and NGOs. As we traveled, I tried to blend into the background: taking portraits of the important officials we met, smiling with laughing children who crowded closer to see their images in the back of my camera, and quietly photographing my travel companions as they furrowed their brows and took thorough notes, intently soaking up information for the articles they would later write.

Author and activist Asha Dornfest was on that trip, and she often teases me about what she observed. "I would watch you as you'd find someone—a doctor, maybe, or a government official—and you'd say, 'May I take your photograph? You have an amazing face!' They would laugh and agree, and then before they knew it, you'd have fired off a few dozen shots, all while asking them questions that made them smile; and then in *seconds*, you'd be done."

At this point in her story, she's usually in the middle of full-on laughter. "You'd thank him and move on, and the guy would be left standing there, stunned, with a goofy grin and a pleased expression of confusion, wondering what just happened, unsure of what they should do next. You had completely charmed them, and they didn't know what to do with that feeling! It was so funny to watch."

It embarrasses me every time Asha tells this story, not because I'm afraid I might have done something wrong—I'm very careful to only photograph people who have given me their full consent—but mostly because I have absolutely no recollection of what Asha is talking about. She'll even give me details of where she witnessed this—exactly who I photographed, and where we were—and it doesn't help. It's as if photography makes me lose all sense of space and time. I become so hyperfocused—on light, on color, and on connecting with the person who has given me the gift of capturing their image—that all else falls away.

My work, in other words, feels like play.

This isn't exaggeration, and there's some science behind this feeling. Stuart Brown is a clinical researcher and founder of the National Institute for Play, a nonprofit committed to bringing the practices and benefits of play into public life. According to Brown in his book *Play: How It Shapes the Brain, Opens the Imagination, and Invigorates the Soul*, play has seven properties. The first is *apparent purposelessness*: play is done simply for its own sake. Second, play is *voluntary*: something that you do simply because you want to do it. There's an *inherent attraction* to play: it's just fun to do and makes you feel good. There's *freedom from time*: you completely lose sense of any passage of time when you're at play. Fifth (and what I was experiencing in Ethiopia), play often results in a *diminished conscious-ness of self*: you're not really concerned about how you look when you're at play, or if you're appearing intelligent or smart; instead, you might describe yourself as being in flow, or "in the zone." Sixth, there's *improvisational potential* with play: there isn't a rigid way of doing what you're doing, and you're free to improvise. And finally, in play there's a *continuation desire*: you want to remain in play and do it over and over again, as long as possible.

Every single one of these properties is true of my photography practice. When I think back to the experience of shooting in Ethiopia, even though it's arguable that my time there wasn't purposeless—I was supposed to be taking those photographs on behalf of ONE, after all—the truth is that even if I wasn't tasked with the goal of taking photographs, I would have done it anyway. Photography is my play.

As it turns out, play can be an integral part of the work we do as activists—and it might even be critical to its success. Stuart Brown's research on play demonstrates a strong correlation between success and play and indicates that play is essential for the development of social as well as problem-solving skills. In fact, early in his career, while conducting research with a group of young men with homi-cidal tendencies, he discovered that what these young men held in common was the *absence* of play in their lives. Furthermore, play, it seems, is important for the cultivation of joy. "It is a critical fact that the opposite of play is not work," explains Brown. "The opposite of play is depression." In her bestselling book *The Gifts of Imperfection*, Brené Brown cites Stuart Brown's work and further expounds on it. "Play helps us foster empathy, helps us navigate complex social groups and is at the core of creativity and innovation," she explains. "Play is an important pillar of living a wholehearted life."

Given what we now know about the benefits of play, it stands to reason that anything that contributes to success and problem-solving, fosters empathy and connection, and nurtures creativity and innovation *has* to be of huge benefit to an activist's work. But the idea that play could be part of activism might seem incongruous. After all, advocacy and activism, almost by definition, require dealing with serious subjects. The activists I interviewed for this book are passionate about ending racism, empowering women and girls, and restoring dignity to those who have been incarcerated. They deal with issues of sexual assault, bigotry, and even violence. Even my own work in Africa was focused on fighting extreme poverty. This is all very serious business. How could any book about activism even entertain the idea of play? And how could we possibly incorporate play into advocacy?

Well, you might remember that in chapter 4, we worked on identifying your light words: the things you would do even if you never got paid for them, the activities that bring you joy no matter the circumstance. It turns out that those light words—in my case, *speak, write, shoot*—hold the key to play. By making a commitment to do these as often as possible, whether in your career or in your activism, you can ensure that play is an integral part of your life. By doing this, your activism may naturally lead to joy.

A great example of this is Aaron Billard—the minister and creative mind behind the Unvirtuous Abbey Twitter account—who plays with social media and humor as part of his advocacy. With his play, he reminds the world that we're all interconnected and called to care for each other—and he does this all while touching on themes of LGBTQ+ rights, climate change, mental health, and so much more. I began following Unvirtuous Abbey years ago, soon after it launched, mostly because its irreverent-yet-love-leading "prayers" appealed to my former-Catholic-girl soul. Some of my favorite Tweets from that time:

> For those who feel ~~forestation~~ frustration with auto-correct, we ~~play~~ pray to the Lord.

> Lord, you who lifted a cup of wine and said, "Remember me," we lift up our Grande Vanilla No-Foam Latte and remember you. Amen.

> Lord, you who told Lazarus to "Come out!" we pray for religious leaders who tell people it's wrong to do that. Amen.

> For those who are living on a prayer. Take our hand. You'll make it. We swear. Amen.

When we met, I asked Aaron why he chose humor and pop culture—two things more often associated with play than with piety—to do his advocacy work.

"Even as a minister, I had attended a number of church services where you could feel the snobbery," he began. "And I don't believe you should ever feel diminished in a service. Also, I used to think my own prayers weren't enough—that in order to be enough, prayers need to be from a prayer book, that kind of thing." He smiled. "I remember when Twitter first started, I started being connected with a lot of other religious people. I'd watch as they'd tweet prayers, and there was a lot of, you know, 'Hasten thou to us this day . . .'" He furrowed his brow. "It was all so pious."

Aaron had always been fascinated by monasticism, but he also loves pop culture and science fiction. "And honestly, snark is my love language," he told me. "So I decided to open an account that was ostensibly created by 'digital monks,' who tweet about pop culture, while reminding followers that they are loved and are called to care for each other. But it was also meant to be an anonymous way to let off steam, to poke fun at the church, and originally, just to be a joke among my friends. But then it took off."

As time went on, more and more people began to feel like they were part of the Abbey—"like they were in on the joke," Aaron told me:

This gives it more meaning, and the result is a community of people who really care about the world. Because for me, it's about humor, it's about poking fun at something that you really care about and love, but never in a mean-spirited way. But also, when something needs to be called out—especially when it's related to the church—I don't hold back. I try to think of myself as a voice of Christianity that's not an overly pious voice, but instead, one that's predominantly caring and real and about love. And it's one of those weird things, Karen, where the Abbey doesn't exist anywhere else except for digitally, and for some reason it's found a home with people in their spirits and in their faith life. Occasionally, I'll get a message from someone who says, "You know, you made me start going back to church." And I just breathe deeply in gratitude.

Perhaps no activist I spoke with embodies the spirit of play more than Brad Montague, the filmmaker behind Kid President.

When we spoke, his book *Becoming Better Grownups* had recently been released, and he giggled as he shared the filing system he'd devised when he was writing. "When I was writing the book, I kept all of my notecards for it in an old *Sesame Street* lunchbox," he laughed, holding up a slightly rusty metallic lunchbox with a faded image of Bert and Ernie on the cover.

I hooted with delight. "That is *awesome.*"

He continued, "It's funny, right? And that helped me not think about the writing of the book as work. It kept me in a playful space." He became more serious:

> But whether I'm writing, or talking with kids, or even speaking with grown-ups, I've found that when you create an atmosphere of levity, you often end with permission to go deeper: to talk about and think about and share really hard things. And when it comes to activism, this permission through levity enables everyone to feel safe, knowing that at any point in time, we can lift out of it. I've found that it's really the most childlike thing in the world to be goofing around and then suddenly talk about death or trauma. Honestly, it's natural. But to make it natural, it means being thoughtful about creating a space to make that happen, and levity and play can do that.

In part, Brad learned this lesson through his work creating the Kid President videos. "The first videos we made were for an audience of young people. It was for an audience of kids who gathered to do a service project in a large gym. We had raised one hundred thousand dollars, and the kids were packing meals and shipping them to different places. It was a really big project."

He smiled and described those early days:

So I decided to make some videos that featured my little brother-in-law, Robby, as if he were a "kid president": the leader of the kids who were gathered. It was just sort of funny and playful—a way to say, "Look what we're all doing; this is a *big deal!*" We wanted to celebrate the fact that they're all young people and at that moment, *they* were the ones in charge. The point was to create the feeling that the grown-ups didn't know or didn't need to know that the kids were the ones who were moving and shaking and making good things happen. We set the tone that the grown-ups can keep doing what they do, complain, and whatever, and that's fine. Facebook is babysitting them, but we kids are going to do some real work right now. So that was the idea.

Eventually Brad and his team put the videos online, and two things happened. First, a lot of teachers started using the videos in their classrooms; that's how the kids started learning about Kid President. Then adults—including parents and college students—began watching the videos as well. Describing this, Brad grew more serious. "I felt like I was walking a tightrope. But the truth is that what's true is true, and what's funny is funny. It's the place where the best stuff exists, when it works for a fourth grader *and* a forty-year-old. *This* was the work."

For both Aaron and Brad, the play *is* the work. That's not the case for all labors of change-making. But even if play can't be the source of your activism, it's still important to include play as an integral part of your life, to ensure that you can return to advocacy with focus and strength. "Play is called recreation because it makes us new again, it re-creates us and our world," writes play researcher Stuart Brown; "a little true play in one's life can bring everything else, including work, back in balance."

In her own work, actor Zuri Adele has witnessed this. To ensure that her character Malika on the show *Good Trouble* is as authentic as possible, Zuri frequently shadows the founders of Black Lives Matter. Her research involves attending actual protests in Los Angeles, but she has also spent time with Black Lives Matter founder Patrisse Cullors and Melina Abdullah, the cofounder of the Los Angeles chapter of Black Lives Matter. When Zuri and I spoke, she marveled that despite the difficult situations that Patrisse and Melina face in their work, they were also careful to weave in moments of joy and play.

"I really admire how much Patrisse and Melina just . . . laugh," she said. "They just love, they dance, they make sure they enjoy their lives." Zuri shook her head as she smiled, thinking about how quickly the activists shift gears. "They'll be laughing and talking shit, and then in the next moment, they're on the phone speaking with a victim's family member, holding space for them because they are devastated by a verdict. Or they'll suddenly realize they need to stop everything to show up at a protest *right* now, knowing full well that at the end of the day, they might be arrested."

I wondered how she saw this playfulness, which she witnessed among the Black Lives Matter founders, as belonging to their activism. As she considered her answer, she grew serious. "Joy is our birthright," she began:

We can only be in this movement from an overflowing cup of energy and presence, and joy and play are part of what fills our cups up. Our ancestors—people who have been fighting for our human rights before us—they passed the baton to us, and we're on a different lap than they were on. They sang and danced and played and created joy, and that's what enabled them to pass the baton to us. So in order for us to be able to pass the baton on, we also have to fill our cups. We can only yell that our lives matter and that we deserve justice if we have the energy to do so.

Zuri grinned. "So I mindfully spend time creating this energy, in order for me to do my work and pursue my own advocacy goals of abolition. Some of it includes calming practice, but other times it includes play. Like dancing unapologetically by myself or with friends. Music is a big part of my play. I just blast music, and I just move."

Zuri and Aaron and Brad teach us that play can bring joy to the work that we do. When advocacy is difficult and challenging, any moments of joy we can curate and cultivate can counterbalance the stress we face in our work. But could play give birth to the creativity and innovation that we need for our advocacy? Is it possible that play not only sustains activism but might even precede it?

My friend Jeff Harry would answer that question with an enthusiastic yes. Jeff is a certified positive psychology coach and play evangelist. He is play personified. He constantly shares videos of himself online doing wacky dances, or shooting baskets, or pushing himself on a scooter through airports. We met at a crowded conference held in the desert in Arizona, where I was drawn to his bowtie made of—wait for it—LEGOs. (Guilty admission: I have a huge weakness for LEGOs and spend an unreasonable amount of time every Christmas tackling a new, enormous LEGO set.) We instantly became friends.

As a coach, Jeff leads workshops with organizations on ways to include play in their workplaces, as well as one-on-one sessions with individuals about how to include play in their lives. I knew he would have some really great insights on the relationship between play and change-making innovation. "First of all," he said, with his trademark energy, "I see play as important as love, sleeping, eating, and breathing."

"That's a strong statement," I responded. "Why do you say that?"

"Well, think about it: when you talk to companies about things like creativity, innovation, and risk-taking—all of those buzzwords—all of those things come from a play mindset. They come from creating a space where you feel safe enough to take a risk and try something that has never been tried before. I think it's ironic that companies are so obsessed with things like 'meeting our numbers' or 'quarterly projections,' when, if you think about when they were first starting out, they were doing the work simply *because it was fun*."

"I love this story about the Wright brothers," he continued, without taking so much as a breath. "The Wright brothers were developing the airplane, right? But there's this story about a second team—apparently funded by a major car company—that hired the best scientists and best engineers and had way more funding. But why did the Wright brothers beat them to the punch? Because they were having fun! They were doing it for fun's sake! And their joy was infectious: folks in their community kept helping them, giving them whatever they needed for their airplane project. The fact that they were first to be airborne doesn't surprise me in the least."

This made sense to me from a business standpoint, but I was curious about his thoughts when it came to advocacy. "So give it to me straight," I said. "How do you see play as an integral part of activism?"

Jeff thought for a second. "Well, I love the quote from author Steven Johnson: 'You'll find the future wherever people are having the most fun.'" Then he continued:

> To create or empower a movement, you must be fully present in the moment. A play mindset can show up whether

you're the first one willing to look silly on the dance floor or the first one to step up against injustice—both are about being boldly present. And being boldly present can make others brave enough to also take risks and push themselves outside of their comfort zone to a place they didn't think possible. This is such an important part of activism. Being the first brave one crashing through the wall is how movements begin. They say the arc of justice is long, and the truth is you may not be around when justice is achieved. But if you find joy in the process and fulfillment in the work, then your work is the foundation upon which justice can be built. No one can take that away from you, regardless of the outcome.

It's a surprising lesson, but play can underpin all of our advocacy work. It can sustain us, re-create us, and provide the source from which our innovation will flow. And done right, it will add joy along the way.

With this, we're well on our way to making light. We're clear on our values and our missions, and we're mindfully listening and creating practices to ensure that not only are we remaining in a beginner's mind, but we're also listening to our own intuition and inner sage. We've even figured out how to create some fun along the way. It's smooth sailing from here on out, right?

Not quite. If activism were that easy, everyone would be brave enough to do it. But as Brené Brown says, when you dare greatly (in activism or not), it's guaranteed that at some point, you'll fall. So how do we ensure that when the challenges arise (and they will), that we can rise with them?

We'll talk about this, and how to celebrate the light we make, in the next section.

PART IV
FIRE AND LIGHT

A Cherokee legend tells of how Grandmother Spider brought light to the world. . . . Using her eight legs, Grandmother Spider made a bowl of clay and wove a web toward the sun. There, she put the sun in her bowl and rolled it home, bringing sunshine to the world.

—Daniel Hume, *Fire Making*

Another world is not only possible, she is on her way. On a quiet day, I can hear her breathing.

—Arundhati Roy

9 | ON SELF-COMPASSION, COURAGE, AND ALIGNING YOUR STAR COLLECTIVE

Houston had a problem.

In the latter part of the 2010s, the city was experiencing an uptick in incidents of hate and bias. This was concerning, and for many, unexpected. Houston was considered one of the most diverse cities in the United States, even displacing New York City in several prominent surveys. Yet according to the *Texas Tribune*, the 2016 presidential campaign and the election of Donald Trump's nationalist political agenda may have emboldened people to express their intolerance more freely. As a result, hostile incidents were on the rise, especially against African American, Jewish, Muslim, and LGBTQ+ citizens.

Alarmed by this increase in hate, a group of more than thirty community-based organizations, institutions, and leaders met in 2017 to develop a plan to reduce incidents of racism and bias. Calling themselves the Houston Coalition Against Hate, they work together toward strengthening the connections among antiracist organizations. As part of their mission, they identify resources within the city for addressing incidents of hate and bias, develop trainings around a common understanding of bias, hate, and the intersectionality of related issues, and collaborate with both local law enforcement and the US Department of Justice to combat racism and bias within the city.

I became aware of the coalition in the latter half of 2019 and was thrilled when I was invited to join the organization. The leadership and its members were impressive, and I was exhilarated by the monthly meetings. At each meeting, after attending to business, one of the member organizations would host an hour-long training session, educating the other members about the issues related to their expertise. For example, one month an organization focused on voting rights shared a presentation on what types of voter suppression they were seeing in the community, and they described what we could do to ensure that every Houston citizen got access to the polls. Another month, an organization focusing on LGBTQ+ equality presented the issues facing the transgender community, educating us all on how to be more trans-inclusive in our day-to-day lives. At still another meeting, a member of the Muslim community told stories of Islamophobia that had occurred in our city and shared ways that we could all be allies. Each month I learn about an issue that I might not have otherwise known about, and I become inspired to make a positive difference in our city.

One month, the featured speaker was the executive director of an immigrants' rights organization. At the time of her presentation, the Trump administration had begun implementing its family separation policy, cracking down on asylum-seekers on the Mexico border. Under this policy, federal authorities separated children from their parents or guardians at the border. The adults were prosecuted for illegal immigration, while the children were placed under the supervision of the US Department of Health and Human

Services. The policy was widely condemned as dehumanizing and cruel, and the speaker detailed the mountain of issues the immigrants' rights community was facing as they attempted to advocate for the families.

As she spoke, she remained poised and calm, clearly articulating her points as she paged through her slide deck. But about five minutes into her presentation, she landed on a slide with a photograph that had been widely shared on social media in previous months. Taken by Getty photographer John Moore, the image depicted a two-year-old asylum-seeker, sobbing, distraught and terrified, as she looked up at an Immigration and Customs Enforcement officer who was searching her mother.

At this point, the speaker broke. "Every time I see this photograph, I lose it," she choked through her tears. "But this little girl is why we do what we do."

She composed herself and continued, but the energy in the room had changed. We remained rapt as we listened to the rest of her presentation, but a sense of determination had settled in the room. We resolved to do whatever we could to help children like the little girl in the photo who had been separated—by our government—from their parents. There was something else too: a surge of empathy for the executive director. Everyone in the room was an activist, and we all knew what it meant to feel the suffering experienced by the people we cared about.

During the question-and-answer portion of the presentation, one of the people in the audience commended the director on her determination and commitment. "It's awe-inspiring to see how much you care about your calling," she said, kindly. "And I hope you're taking care of yourself too. This is difficult work."

"I know," the director returned her smile. "I need to be better at that."

The truth is that we could all improve our self-care. But when we talk about activism and advocacy, the idea of focusing on self seems completely counterintuitive. Activism is other-centered. Taking care of ourselves as activists might mean we have less time and energy for the people for whose rights we are fighting. Wouldn't that be selfish?

◆ ◆ ◆

One of the attendees of that immigrants' rights session was Sean Fitzpatrick, the executive director of the Jung Center. As both a clinical psychologist and theologian, he understands deeply how helping others can have a detrimental effect on our own psyche if we aren't mindful about caring for ourselves. As part of his work, he serves activists and other social justice advocates, ensuring they protect their mental health; he gave a presentation for the Houston Coalition Against Hate on just this subject. Sean came to this work partly as a result of an experience he had as a young therapist, his first session with someone who was suicidal.

"I was completely overwhelmed," he told me. "My distress was about my client, of course, and an empathic response to her story, but it was also about the fact that I didn't have what I needed to take care of her. I was also really worried about *myself* and what might happen to me if she attempted suicide."

At this, Sean took a deep breath. Then he continued,

So I went home, and instead of having the one beer that I would have normally had while I cooked dinner, I fixed myself a stiff drink. It was more than just a shot in a glass— I had a massive Jack Daniels whiskey with Coke. And I got drunk. But not just drunk; *puking* drunk. And that was *completely* unlike me. It never happened again, because the lesson for me in that moment—one which I've been trying to integrate ever since—is that being connected to suffering profoundly affects you as a human being, and you have to pay attention to that. Being connected to suffering is part of what we endure as therapists, but also what we endure as activists. We have to pay attention to the effect it's having on us, so that we can continuing being present in our work on an ongoing basis.

I furrowed my brow. "You know what's weird, then?" I spoke slowly, measuring my words. "It's weird that people get into activism *at all*. I mean, if being connected to suffering can have a harsh effect on us, you'd think that we'd develop an everyone-for-themselves mentality, right?"

"Well . . . it's not that simple," he smiled.

The reason that people are motivated to do this work is because of how personally invested we are in each other. We're wired for connection, and as a result, our empathy for each other is activated. As humans, we have a primal need to help. But—and this is the thing—the other side of that interconnection is that if left unchecked, repeated exposure to trauma will result in our own bodies shutting down. Our souls will shut down. And that can take the form of not being able to get out of bed in the morning. Or it can take the form of substance abuse. Or decreased productivity. All kinds of things. Something else kicks in to protect you, and that means you're no longer able to do the work anymore.

"Well, you're just full of good news, aren't you?" I frowned. "This sound pretty awful. I say we should just stop helping people altogether."

Sean laughed. "Well, this is why taking care of ourselves needs to be an integral and nonnegotiable part of advocacy and activism." He became more animated. "It's like that great Audre Lorde quote, from a book of essays she wrote called *A Burst of Light*, where she said, 'Caring for myself is not self-indulgence, it is self-preservation, and that is an act of political warfare.'"

At the time she wrote that book, Sean told me, Lorde was undergoing treatment for cancer. But she understood something crucial: "She understood that her voice was an access point for the populations and people who were voiceless," Sean explained. "She knew that her determination to remain in the world and stay in the work was an act of political warfare, because it would allow her to continue the political fight. If we're going to do the work, we have to make sure that we care for ourselves so that we maintain the *capacity* to do the work."

Author, activist, and faith leader Valarie Kaur is also a fan of Audre Lorde's work, and she sees caring for ourselves as one of the most important things we can do when it comes to activism. "Loving ourselves is frontline social justice work," she said. "There's no need for us to suffer in order to serve."

When I asked Valarie how we do that, she answered immediately. "In the words of Angela Davis, it's about 'longevity,'" she began. Then she referenced the midwife metaphor that she often uses when speaking of activism and advocacy. "In any long labor—the labor of birthing, the labor of making a life, the labor of remaking of a nation—the wisdom of the midwife is that there's a rhythm to the labor. It's not 'Breathe once, and then push the rest of the way.' It's breathing and then pushing, and then breathing again. It's something I'm still learning. My task is to figure out the rhythms in a day, in a week, in a month, in a year, in a season of life, that allow me to breathe and push."

"So how do you figure out those rhythms?" I asked.

"Well, it's a practice, right?" she explained. "You need to figure out which practices your body wants, whether it's writing, resting, practicing gratitude, dancing, meditation—whatever. And when you figure out what those practices are, then you think in rhythms—what can I do every day? Every week? Weaving these rhythms into our lives is how we can ensure that we're loving ourselves as a matter of course."

Valarie's words reminded me of my coaching training with the Wholebeing Institute. As we saw in chapter 2, positive psychology is the scientific study of the positive aspects of the human experience that make life worth living. According to the positive psychology research of the Wholebeing Institute, people who thrive take care of themselves in five ways:

They focus on cultivating *spirituality* in their lives by ensuring they're leading meaningful lives, and mindfully savoring the present.

They take care of their *physical* bodies, especially for the purpose of tapping into the connection between their minds and their bodies.

They are intentional about *intellectual* stimulation by engaging in deep learning and remaining open to new experiences.

They nurture constructive *relationships*, both with themselves and with others.

And finally, they're not afraid of their *emotions*; they don't deny or suppress their feelings but are mindful of them.

These five practices—captured with the acronym SPIRE—help us cultivate a practice of positivity. At first blush, this all seems pretty obvious. Of *course* these spiritual, physical, intellectual, relational, and emotional practices would naturally lead to a more joyful life. But let's be honest: cultivating all five elements of well-being seem incredibly overwhelming. I mean, seriously, who has the time? Say I spend an hour meditating and another hour at the gym each day. Then I add in some solid time educating myself by reading a book or taking an online course. After that, I'd need to add some quality time with my husband and daughter and friends. Of course, I can't forget to sit with my emotions every single day. And I must make a point of getting eight hours of sleep every night. After doing all of this, when, exactly, would I earn a living, to speak nothing of actually advocating for others? Besides, at some point I'd need to clean my house. Or, you know, shower.

It's during these moments of overwhelm that we need to remember Valarie's advice of listening to our bodies and our emotions to determine what they need and in what rhythm. In other words, *these aren't goals you need to achieve every single day.* Maybe you only do some of these things several days a week. Or one day a week. Or just once a month. And perhaps you can weave a couple of them *throughout* your day, like stopping every few hours to do a few yoga stretches or spending a few meditative moments at your desk. Recall that so much of what we do as activists is about *practice*, and that includes the self-care we undertake in order to ensure that we can keep showing up.

In chapter 8, I shared a practice to ensure that we mindfully set intentions for our days. One of those intentions specifically invites introspection and checking in with your mental and physical health and self-care. This practice is forward-looking: the intentions are for the day ahead. But there's a second practice—a *reflective* one—that is helpful and that involves tracking how you're actually doing, one that you can do at the end of the day. I've devised a quick little tracker in my journal, where I simply color in blocks that represent each of those self-care traits in the SPIRE model: spirituality, physical health, intellectual curiosity, relational cultivation, and emotional care. Before I go to bed, I ask myself: How did I manage to care for each of these areas during the day? And then I fill in the blocks.

Used over time, this tracker can tell you where you might need to focus your intentions the following day to ensure that the colors on the tracker are balanced. I've included a sample tracker in the The Lightmaker's Manual toward the back of this book for your inspiration. It's a simple way for you to ensure that your self-care remains as important as the rest of the tasks that you've set yourself over the month.

Of course, despite your best self-care intentions, there will be times when you find yourself feeling especially anxious, maybe even like my friend Sean was when he spiraled into his own distress as he cared for his client. Let's face it: sometimes activism and caregiving will knock you flat. So how do you catch your breath long enough to make mindful decisions, rooted in self-care?

◆ ◆ ◆

Kristin Neff, a professor at the University of Texas, has been credited with conducting the very first academic studies in the world on the subject of self-compassion. A Buddhist, she describes self-compassion exactly the way you and I would probably describe it even without academic research; that is, self-compassion is treating yourself as you would treat a good friend. According to Dr. Neff, people who practice self-compassion are far more productive, make better partners, parent better, live longer, and heal faster. Neff offers a tool to help us be more self-compassionate when we're suffering. (For the record, "suffering" can include anything from the pain you feel on behalf of the community for which you're advocating to stubbing your toe.) The tool is a *self-compassion break.*

Neff posits that true self-compassion is composed of three elements: *mindfulness* (bringing your awareness to what you're feeling and what is happening in the moment), *common humanity* (reminding yourself that we are all human and thus interconnected), and *kindness* (self-explanatory). A self-compassion break involves combining all three of these elements in a moment when you've had the wind knocked out of you.

It works like this: when something has happened that is causing you pain, first, sit with your eyes closed. Become aware of your breathing. Then think about what is causing you discomfort. It could be something you're worrying about, or physical pain you're experiencing, or even a specific sadness. As you're focusing on this, you think to yourself: "This is hard." This is the *mindfulness* part: spending a moment feeling your pain. It's like if I came to you and told you I was going through a hard time, you would listen and probably say something like, "That must be so hard, Karen." Instead of immediately going into fix-it mode, you acknowledge the feeling. Offer yourself the same care you'd show to me. This is you showing empathy to yourself.

Second, after you've sat with this for a moment, say to yourself, "But you know what? This feeling is part of what it means to be human. It's normal and natural to feel this way." This is the *common humanity* part. This stage helps you realize, in the moment, that *you are not alone.* This feeling, this pain, is part of life, and it is okay to feel it. You are not being punished; rather, feeling what you are feeling is simply part of living.

Then, finally, after you acknowledge that what you're feeling is a totally normal part of being human, you say, "May I be kind to myself." This is the *kindness* part. This is you telling yourself—or God, or Allah, or the universe, or whomever—that you want to be gentle with yourself as you move through your pain.

A self-compassion break only takes a few minutes. It's about taking a beat and getting centered. And Dr. Neff's research has found that when you've grounded yourself by doing these three steps, you detach a bit from the pain, maybe even gain some clarity about your next move. A self-compassion break is all about being kind to yourself, allowing yourself to become calm so you don't move in panic. I used self-compassion breaks constantly in the aftermath of Hurricane Harvey. Those short moments made all the difference in my decision-making and mental health during that time.

Here's the upshot: whether you track your acts of self-care with the SPIRE tool or take self-compassion breaks, you must pay attention to your own mental and physical health. To be an activist over the long haul, you need to do this in an almost ritualistic, rhythmic way. Keep checking in with yourself. As the late poet Mary Oliver said, "Attention is the beginning of devotion." By paying attention to our own emotional, mental, and physical health in a rhythmic manner, we ensure our own longevity in the work of change at hand.

◆ ◆ ◆

Several years ago, I moderated a panel at a conference for young entrepreneurs. After the panel, I sat with four young women during a mentorship session, in which they asked questions and I answered as best I could. One woman asked me if I had a mentor.

"Huh," I said, and I thought for a moment. "I don't think I have a mentor. I think of mentors as people who are older or more experienced in what you do, who have already blazed the path you're about to take. Because I do a hodgepodge of all kinds of stuff, I can't think of many people who are both older than me and who have done the same work."

I spoke slowly, scrambling for an answer that might be helpful, something that the young woman could implement in her own life. Suddenly it came to me. I said brightly, "But I *do* have a war council."

She blinked, and looked vaguely alarmed. I guess *war council* is a pretty aggressive term. I explained what I meant, and gradually the furrows between her brows relaxed, and she got it. Since that time, I've thought better of that term and replaced it with one that feels more accurate (and less like I'm planning an insurgency): a *star collective*. And I'm convinced that everyone—most especially activists—needs one.

Brené Brown says that as much as we'd like to pretend that we don't care what anyone thinks, it's a lie: we actually *do* care what people think, because we're neurobiologically wired for connection. Given this, we should strive for being absolutely clear on *whose* opinion matters. In fact, I've heard her recommend an exercise in which you draw a one-inch-by-one-inch square on a piece of paper and then, inside the box, write the names of people whose opinions matter to you. If, for any reason, you need more room, it's time to cull some names, because the people whose names are in the box should fill some very specific criteria. I agree. There are very few friends and family members whose names I write in my own little box. These folks are special, and their friendship and advice and counsel have been instrumental in helping me make life decisions: from marriage to parenting to everything in between. I can't imagine going through life without them.

The people in my star collective—formerly known as my war council—are similar to these one-inch-box friends, but also slightly different. My star collective is a very specific group of friends and advisors, and we turn to each other specifically for work and advocacy advice. Over the years, the members of my star collective have changed. Some have been men, some have been women. Some have been older, and some have been younger. Some of them knew each other, and some never met. But in every case, these are folks with whom I have a special relationship and whose advice I value. Through my conversations, I discovered that many activists have a group of people on whom they rely to make sure that they are staying on course. Call them your star collective, your team, your tribe, your war council: no matter what you call this group, it's essential for longevity in activism.

"Having a team is super-important," Brené told me emphatically. "We talk through everything—*we talk through everything*—and they don't pull punches. They'll say to me, 'You're burned out,' or 'You're not being productive,' or even 'You're posting stuff online that is outside of your values. Take a break.' They are people who I trust and who have my best interests at heart. They're people who know me, and I listen to them."

Activist Tarana Burke also relies deeply on her star collective for support and advice. Tarana's activism journey is unusual, in that she'd been working tirelessly as an advocate for sexual assault survivors for more than a decade before a chance tweet from actor Alyssa Milano launched her Me Too movement into international renown. Her sudden fame was disorienting.

"I can say without hyperbole that these friends absolutely saved me and kept me afloat since everything exploded, not unlike the ways that they had done so in the past," Tarana shared. "From the moment #MeToo went viral—and I mean, *the very day*—these friends have given me grounding and perspective. I remember when I was witnessing everything happen across the internet, and I was freaking out, one of my best girlfriends said—very calmly and very assuredly—'You have been doing this for so long. *Everyone* knows that. No one can take away what is yours. Just pull out your receipts.' It was that moment that gave me the calm and perspective to see my way forward. And they've always been that way with me."

Similarly, artist Jordan Seaberry shared a moment when a member of his star collective convinced him that he needed to return to the Rhode Island School of Design to finish his art degree. He had dropped out of school and hadn't created any art since that time. "I'd been out of school for about two years," he remembered, "and I really convinced myself I wouldn't ever need to go back to school, and didn't really want to. It was my best friend who forced me to return." He smiled at the memory. "She knew that as much as I was enjoying the activism work that I *was* doing, I was still feeling alone. She knew that I wasn't nourishing myself, and I was burning the candle at both ends." His friend got direct:

So she sat me down and said, "We are doing a life retreat. We are going to break your life up into categories, and we're going to figure out what you want from each of them." She took a big sheet of paper, and she split my life up. One was career, one was education, one was health, one was relationships—I can't remember all of them. But she forced me to reflect on what my goals were for each of these areas of my life. We worked together for about three hours. When we were finished, I sat back and said, "Well . . . *shit*. I guess I gotta go back to school."

A star collective might seem like a nice but nonessential aspect of activism. But Valarie Kaur maintains that having a group of friends to hold you accountable is not only a form of self-care; it's an essential tool for activists and advocates. "We don't give birth alone, and we don't go to battle alone," she explained. Valarie often speaks of "revolutionary love"—a commitment to fight for justice through the ethic of love—as a foundational requirement of all advocacy and activism work. For this reason, she believes that culti vating a star collective—what she calls her "pocket"—helps us stay rooted in that foundation.

"I believe that revolutions not only happen in these big grand public moments, but in the places where people are coming together to inhabit this new way of being," she explained. And then she continued, "When we show up with love in invisible, behind-closed-doors, one-on-one spaces, we are practicing a way of being in community. And we can take those hard-earned lessons—about how to love others, our opponents, and ourselves—into our activism. I've come to see my life as a series of experiments with revolutionary love. Personal or political, the ethic of love is the same, right? So my relationships enable me to do the activism work out in the world with some intimately earned wisdom behind it."

Cultivating a star collective isn't easy; after all, your star collective should be a pretty elite group. Not every friend, great as they might be, is necessarily star collective material. Because you will be looking to these folks for advice related to advocacy work, these need to be people whose own work and ethic you believe in. In other words, they need to embody the advocacy ethic that you're trying to create for yourself. But there are other traits—eight of them, actually—that they should also share to earn a spot on your star collective.

First, the folks in your star collective should *know you well*. They don't need to have known you for a long time, but they need to know your strengths and your weaknesses, your passions, and what you don't suffer well. You trust them to give you insight and advice, because they have a pretty good idea how you're likely to react to the consequences of any decisions make.

Second, each member of your star collective should *fully understand your work*. They should understand why you do the advocacy work that you do, what you hope to achieve through your efforts, and your personal mission and values. The members of your star collective don't need to share the same mission or do the same work, but they need to *get it*. They deeply understand your goals and fully support them.

Third, when you find success in your activism, the members of your star collective should *be genuinely, no-foolin' happy for you*. These folks don't have petty jealousies or find passive-aggressive ways to tear you down. These aren't people who, when your work is effective, lament that they never have success in their own work. Their first inclination is to celebrate you when something great happens, even if (and perhaps *especially* if) you don't necessarily see reason to celebrate. They insist that you stop and acknowledge your wins. (Relatedly, when something good happens to *them*, they're interested in sharing that success with you—but in a way that includes you in their celebration, not in a way that feels competitive or belittling.)

Fourth, the members of your star collective should *genuinely want to help when you fail*. In advocacy and activism work, there will be many opportunities to fall. We may be overcome with discouragement, or hopelessness, or a sense of failure. In these moments, we need people around us who will remind us that we don't do this alone. Valarie Kaur shared, "I used to think that my breathlessness—those moments when I felt so overwhelmed, so paralyzed, so helpless—I used to think those moments were a sign of my weakness. But one of the people who is in my close circle told me, 'Oh no, no, no, my love—your breathlessness is a sign of your bravery. It means you are awake to what's happening in the world right now.'" Valarie said that he reminded her that "it's okay to feel everything I'm feeling, and the key is to breathe, to let breath in your body. And then my circle helped me find the one thing I could do to show up in the next moment."

Aaron Billard, the creative mind behind Unvirtuous Abbey, calls certain members of his star collective his "edgewalkers." "These are the people who will go to the edge with you when you're struggling, and look over the edge with you, and talk with you about it, and listen to you," explained Aaron. "Then they'll help walk you back away from the edge. These are the people I trust when I'm ready to torch everything. These are the ones who approach me with kindness and say, 'Okay, let's look at this together.'"

This is important: the edgewalker members of your star collective are the folks who will listen with care when you grieve about something going wrong in advocacy work and will allow you some time to process it. Yet they also won't allow you to wallow. They'll let you know if you're being overdramatic, and they'll help you find the steps needed to rise again. They are, in a word, indispensable.

Fifth, your star collective members should *not be afraid of telling you if you're screwing up*. It's not all boosting and pom-poms: while they're supportive, they're also practical. Remember, Brené counts on her star collective to clearly tell her when she's living outside of her values. She trusts them implicitly, which she wouldn't be able to do if the members of her collective were purely her cheerleaders. Members of a star collective are kind, but they are firm. They should tell you if something isn't a great idea and help walk you through the thought process behind your idea to determine if there's a way to make it better. They tell you if you're about to do something that doesn't reflect the values that you hold deeply and help you reconsider any steps as needed.

Sixth, you should implicitly *trust the people in your star collective.* When you speak with them, it's vault time. They keep secrets secret, without a second thought. These are the people you know who don't share the secrets they keep for *others* either; they don't tell you stories you don't have the right to know, so you know they're treating what you confidentially share with them with the same consideration. They're also willing to be vulnerable with you when you're vulnerable with them.

Seventh, the members of your star collective *shouldn't have any skin in your game.* This is important. No matter how incredibly giving or generous or honorable they might be, people who do such similar work that they might end up competing with you for future opportunities or grants or anything else might not be eligible candidates for your collective. Unlike the roles a mentor might play, the people in your star collective should have no conflicts of interest in giving you advice.

And finally, the members of your star collective should *always have your best interests at heart.* This is a nonnegotiable.

That's quite a list, isn't it? Let's face it: even knowing one person who fits all eight traits is a total gift! Yet you may be surprised, as you reflect on your relationships, by how many people in your life could fit the bill. There isn't a set number of people you should have on your star collective, but I'm a fan of having multiple members. Right now, there are a handful of people in mine, and this feels perfect. Each person has a different superpower, and whenever I'm dealing with a sticky situation, they each bring their own lenses, experiences, skills, and gifts to bear on my challenge. While the members of my star collective know each other, sometimes I call a particular member for a one-on-one conversation, because I know that their specific gifts would be particularly helpful to me. In any event, don't worry: a single-person star collective (a lone star, perhaps?) can work beautifully, and it's a great place to start.

Once you've determined who should be in your star collective, the trick is figuring out their care and feeding. In other words, once you've found people who share the characteristics above, how do you craft a star-collective relationship with them?

In my experience, the relationship can be formal or informal. Your star collective meetings can be completely organic: you could simply call someone whose advice you value and say, "Hey, I think you and I have similar ideology when it comes to goals and how we want to give back in our lives. If you're up for it, I'd love to meet you for coffee occasionally, and we can act as a sounding board for each other." And then make sure to *follow through*: make the coffees happen. If you and your star collective friend or friends aren't in the same city, no worries: there are tons of free videoconferencing options to make connection happen. The point is just to *make it happen.*

Or your meetings could have more structure: my star collective and I schedule time together via videoconference, and have from the start, because we live all over the United States. Someone will send a group email and say, "Hey, it's been a while, can we check in with each other and see how we can all help each other?" And then we get something on the calendar. Once we connect, we take turns talking about what we're working on and specifically what we're hoping to get advice on. We have time limits, so we ensure that no one person monopolizes the time we have together.

One time we happened to be attending the same conference. We knew we would each be busy while we were there: a couple of us were speaking at the conference, a few of us had meetings scheduled, and each of us wanted to network with other attendees. We knew our time together was going to be scarce, so we got creative. My star collective friends flew to Houston ahead of time and road-tripped with me to the conference. In the two-and-a-half-hour journey, we divvied up the time to have a star collective meeting en route: one person took notes while I drove, and we took turns sharing the challenges we were facing as we worked for change in our various roles. Before we'd even checked into our hotel, the notetaker had texted us photos of her notes to each of us, so we would have record of the wisdom that each had shared with us. By the time we dumped our bags in our hotel rooms and headed into the conference, we were completely energized.

This brings up my final point: one of the biggest rules of the star collective relationship is that you have to give as good as you get. The eight traits of star collective members *must* be traits that you are also committed to bringing to the relationship: the ability to celebrate your friend's successes, to put competitiveness on the back burner, to be a source of complete trust and care for your friend's advocacy work, and so on. If, after some soul searching, you know that you cannot provide that level of care for a particular person, then they're probably not a good candidate for your collective. This relationship has to be mutually beneficial.

My friend Asha Dornfest, who happens to be one of the members of my star collective, sums up why maintaining these relationships is such a critical part of activism: "Your star collective can provide reality checks around you," she explains, "and having loving people helping you with course correction is really important, especially in advocacy. Also, the truth is that activism can be so lonely. Sometimes you spend a lot of time talking to the void, to people who don't agree with you. You *have* to have some joy and support and lightness and levity along the way. Thankfully, that's what your people can provide for you."

Self-compassion and self-care are important, and your star collective ensures that you're receiving external support for the work you do and the advocacy in which you engage. By creating an atmosphere of compassion, both through self-care and community, you'll set the stage for you to fully engage in changing the world—and access joy along the way.

10 | ON CURIOSITY, VISION BOARDS, AND EXPECTING TO FAIL

When I finally left my law practice, I promised myself that I was going to "follow my bliss." Life was too short, I thought, to do anything that didn't make me happy. By that time, I'd already had a pretty robust photography practice—and the photoblog to prove it—so I decided to become a professional photographer. I let people know that I was officially available for hire. Almost immediately people started contacting me to do their headshots, photograph their weddings, and document their major life events. I was, it seemed, off to the races.

And? I hated it.

The pressure of photographing someone's wedding was overwhelming. The deadlines I had to work under to get a full set of photographs to my client felt like a chore. And frankly, the requests people made for editing the photographs annoyed me: *No, I will not remove your laugh lines, or your beauty mark, or the apparent extra thirty pounds of weight you think you're carrying, just because you perceive yourself to be unattractive*, I'd fume to myself. *You're beautiful!* The longer I sat in front of my computer, editing my images to meet the criteria of my clients by deadline, the more resentful I grew. I began to wonder whether I actually enjoyed photography after all.

So as abruptly as I began, I stopped taking clients. I began shooting for fun again, trying my hand at a photojournalistic approach. I started thinking about photography as a type of storytelling. And slowly, frame by frame, I rekindled my love for my practice. I shared my stories and images online, and I became obsessed with using photography to tell stories and using images to illustrate the diverse beauty of the world. Then the ONE Campaign came calling, asking me to use my now-developed photojournalistic skills to fight poverty. The rest, as they say, is history.

In my journey to follow my bliss, I had inadvertently stumbled upon a better code to live by—one that I only heard expressed years later while listening to a podcast. The guest, author Elizabeth Gilbert, said something that struck me as so on-the-money that it stopped me dead in my tracks. "Don't follow your passion," she said, "follow your *curiosity*."

Following your curiosity is such a radical shift in mindset for most people and one that can change everything. "Follow your bliss" and "follow your passion" only make sense if you really understand what your bliss is. But most of us haven't figured that out yet. Or even if you think you've figured it out, your bliss will change. Your passion will morph. What seems like a passion now may wane in the future—and honestly, I think that's fine. Having a single passion your entire life is like knowing from a very young age what you want to be when you grow up: amazing if it happens, but simply not the case for most people. And the only way you'll discover your bliss or your passion is by remaining open and curious. This is especially true when it comes to activism and advocacy.

Filmmaker and Kid President creator Brad Montague received similar advice when speaking with the spouse of a hero of his, the late Fred Rogers, host of the educational children's television series *Mister Rogers' Neighborhood.* You must first understand how big a deal it is to Brad that he was able to speak to Fred Rogers's wife. Brad's mission in life is to help kids understand that their voices matter—a concept that was core to Fred Rogers's work.

"*Mister Rogers' Neighborhood* was a staple of my earliest child-hood," Brad writes in *Becoming Better Grownups.* "For years I thought he was speaking directly to me. I've since learned that was part of his gift, as millions of other children felt the exact same way. By seeing how he proceeded through life in our daily television neighborhood visits, I gained a better understanding of how I fit locally in my neighborhood—just by being me. As I've grown, I've come to understand it has equal bearing on how I move in the world as a global neighbor."

When I met Brad, his eyes lit up at the memory of his conversation with Joanne Rogers, Fred Rogers's widow. He shared with me how the best advice she gave him was about following your curiosity. "Meeting Joanne Rogers was such a thrill," he told me, grinning at the memory, "and I was able to ask her so many questions. Like, 'How did he know what to do? How did he know he was on the right path?'" Brad paused, then said,

> She smiled at me, and said, "Honey, he *never* knew. *He never knew.* At first, he thought he was going into ministry; that didn't work out. Then, he thought he would go into television to make *that* a ministry, and it was a mess, so he left television. And then he went into something for older people, and then he realized he wanted and needed to go back to kids. He described his whole career as a 'guided drift.' Eventually, he was able to look back on his life and see that each experience uniquely prepared him for the next one."

Brad smiled. "I loved this, and it's a story I'm holding onto with my own life."

♦ ♦ ♦

Mr. Rogers's concept of "guided drift" reminded me of Sean Fitzpatrick's words: that spiritual experience is accidental, and that spiritual practice makes you accident-prone. I began to wonder if the lightmakers I interviewed had practices that helped them to pay attention to their own "drift"—and whether they felt like it was being "guided." One of the first people I asked was my friend Jess Weiner, whose lifelong mission has been in diversity, inclusion, and women and girls' empowerment. It turns out she has also made a habit of intentional curiosity. Jess says she is "culturally Jewish more than religiously Jewish," but she still believes in a God, she told me, and being in connection to "lots of helpers."

"I always felt there was a community of guidance," she explained. "Maybe ancestors, maybe angels, spirits—that sort of thing. There's a saying that I've always loved: 'coincidence is just God's way of remaining anonymous.' So I pay attention. I've always been curious. And just by following these bread crumbs, these coincidences, I've been able to create this life of activism and advocacy."

I was eager to hear more. "So, how do you pay attention, then?" I asked. "Do you have any practices that help you stay curious?"

"I do vision boards religiously," was Jess's immediate response. I nodded in recognition. I'm a fan of vision boards: those collections of images that offer a visual representation of what you hope to create in your life. Making a vision board can be a deeply meditative practice, in which you imagine goals, hopes, and longings by creating a collage of pictures and words. I've made mine once a year or so as a way to reflect on the year ahead, but I had never considered doing them more often than that.

"I do vision boards every six months if I can," Jess continued. "I do a big one once a year, and it stays up in my office. And then I do every-six-month ones that live in my closet, so that when I get dressed in the mornings, I can see them. Sometimes my vision boards are less about goals and more about feelings or ideals that I want to attract or I'm curious about."

I asked Jess how vision boards help her, and she admitted that she found the process of gathering and collecting her images to feel spiritual in nature. "I don't go in the process of making my vision boards with any sort of plan; instead, I see what calls to me. Those guides—those helpers I mentioned earlier—I say a little prayer to them, something like, 'Show me what I need to see, reveal to me what I need to think about.' And then I begin. It sets an intention of curiosity for me to see what emerges."

Actor, activist, and griot Zuri Adele also has a committed vision board practice that she uses to awaken her curiosity. And for her, the process is ongoing. "I have a vision board that I started seven years ago, and I just keep adding to it," she shared. "And so now it's layers thick. I take all images that speak to me from magazines or publications or online, and then I just lay them all out. I usually look for where I see myself, or just something that resonates and inspires curiosity. I trust my instincts even if I don't know why, but simply trusting my eye and my spirit, I select them for my board."

After speaking with Jess and Zuri, I created my own vision board specifically related to the activism and advocacy that I wish to pursue. I've found that this vision board not only helps me to clarify how I want my advocacy to look; it's a tool I can use to monitor my progress, assess whether it seems true to mission, and inspire curiosity about my own work. An activist vision board can help you experiment with harnessing your skills to make a difference. I call my current vision board a "living vision board" because, like Zuri, I'll modify and add to it over time. Creating a vision board can be a particularly clarifying exercise, helping to unearth interests you might want to explore in the future.

In "The Lightmaker's Manual" toward the back of this book, I share my living vision board process. Perhaps it will inspire you to create your own vision board. Doing so is a wonderful way to practice curiosity, with a constant mindset of experimentation. Enjoy the process. And then return to your vision board in the coming months and years to adjust as necessary. Enjoy where your curiosity and experimentation take you.

Speaking of experimentation, there's something inherent in the concept of "experimenting" that normalizes the concept of failure. Activism and advocacy are, of course, fraught with opportunities to fail, and cultivating an experimentation outlook can help develop your own resilience. For this reason, I advocate making a practice of experimentation a part of your day-to-day life.

This is a lesson I learned from a documentary I watched some time ago. The documentary itself was only mildly interesting, but one of the interview subjects said something really striking: he was discussing the part that failure has played in his success as a writer, and while he said that he'd failed more times in life than he could remember, he also said this: that to be creative, you have to be *willing* to fail. In his mind, you needed not only to accept that failure is part of creativity but actually have the courage to walk into any new creative practice knowing full well that you are going to fail.

And you must do so without a shred of embarrassment or self-consciousness. You have to go into any new practice with a learner's mind: being sure that what you're doing isn't going to work but willing to experiment. As you begin anything new, you have to both assume that you'll fail and that you'll learn something new that will help you improve.

It makes sense, if you think about it. There are innumerable stories of the greatest inventors of the world failing constantly before finally creating the innovation that transforms our lives. A beginner's—or learner's—mind was crucial to their success, and we've already established that it's essential to any advocacy practice. For this reason, I decided to see if a practice of experimentation would be helpful in the development of my own resilience. So I began a sketching practice around the same time I started writing this book.

It all started because of the tiny sketchbook my husband, Marcus, put in my Christmas stocking. I cannot stress enough how out of character it is for me to begin sketching. Up until very recently, I held a deep-seated belief that I *could. not. draw.* I've never taken a drawing class in my life, save for a year of drafting in engineering school. And in drafting there are so many tools—straightedges and protractors and triangles—that while I became proficient in *engineering* drawing, I still believed deeply that I was missing the sketch gene.

But something about being given that sketchbook gave me permission to fail. I would have *never* bought a sketchbook for myself, but having been given it . . . well, I *had* to use it, right? So I went into this little practice fully intending to make truly horrible art. My only rule for myself was that I had to freehand everything. There would be no relying on the T-squares and straightedges and protractors of engineering school; I simply had to eyeball everything I drew. My daughter Alex, who is a talented artist, told me, "Just sketch everything with a pencil and eraser until you like what you've done, and then paint it, and then outline it with pen." I took this advice to heart.

I intended to simply draw things I found around the house, but sometimes I used photographs I'd taken in the past as references. My only goal was to see if I could sketch a likeness of whatever was in front of me. I had absolutely no intention of sharing anything I drew with anyone; this was just going to be an experimental, meditative practice that I would do while binge-watching a Netflix show or winding down my weekdays. I honestly didn't even expect improvement; the most I was going for was *enjoyment*.

Believe me: I am not proud of every sketch I do. (A recent sketch of three nail polish bottles was seriously abysmal.) But while I don't think the Louvre will be banging on my door anytime soon, the majority of my sketches at least *resemble* their real-life counterparts. And honestly, that is something I never expected to happen. But when you walk into a venture with a mind devoted to curiosity and experimentation, coupled with persistence and tenacity and most importantly *the expectation of failure*—well, somehow, that mindset improbably yields results.

This is the same with activism. Following our curiosity, envisioning our ways forward, all with a mindset of experimentation: in a field fraught with disappointment, these things bring light. Of course we will fail. Of course we will need to give ourselves countless self-compassion breaks and rely on our star collectives to pick us up and dust us off. But curiosity, experimentation, persistence, tenacity, and the expectation of failure will yield results. You will learn, pivot, adjust, and achieve. It's the physics of curiosity. And like all laws of the universe, it is immutable.

11 | ON GRATITUDE AND CELEBRATION

In the opinion of virtually anyone who was paying attention, the year 2020 was a particularly difficult one. There were environmental disasters. Rampant racial discrimination. Political protests against police killings of unarmed Black people frequently ended in violence. There were earthquakes. Economies crashed. The earth's temperature grew hotter than ever. Even the animals seemed angry: "murder hornets," which reportedly deliver a sting equivalent to three to ten yellow jackets attacking at once, invaded North America. And then, God help me, there were the "meth gators": authorities in Loretto, Tennessee, became concerned that alligators, consuming methamphetamines that had been flushed down toilets, were becoming alarmingly aggressive. All of these things, by the way, happened while the planet was wrapped in the smothering effects of a virulent and global pandemic.

And this was all before *September*.

So no one could fault you if you complained about the challenges of 2020. Yet kvetching about how horrible a year it has been was a normal pastime way before 2020. Let's be honest: come December of any given year, when folks ask us how we're doing, inevitably we launch into a complaint about how busy things have been and how overwhelmed we feel. Exhaustion is viewed as the hallmark of a productive life. The news media continues to highlight one heartbreaking event after another. When we look back at the end of any given year, it can seem like there was no good in it at all.

But without minimizing any challenges life throws at us, I maintain we can exacerbate these hardships by focusing on the difficult rather than the good. I contend that even among all of the despair and heartache, life gives us a helping of good as well. As 2020 drew to a close, for example, one of my coaching clients confided in me with no small amount of shock: "It sounds weird to say this, but this year has taught me so much about what I'm capable of. I'm really enjoying coming into my own."

What my client had stumbled upon was the fact that even in challenging times, there are still moments of good; even more incredibly, it's possible to maintain hope. It's not easy, but with mindfulness and the intentional nurturing of optimism and positivity, growth and goodness can result. And a huge part of that mindful practice optimism is the expression of gratitude.

Expressing gratitude is intrinsic to cultivating joy. Brené Brown has found this connection in her own extensive research. "Without exception," she says, "every person I interviewed who described living a joyful life or who described themselves as joyful, actively practiced gratitude and attributed their joyfulness to their gratitude practice." Brené has used string lights as a metaphor for the relationship between joy and gratitude: if each light represents a moment of gratitude, looking back over time, the evidence of joy is shown on when you look at the lights—or life as a whole. Further, Brené describes both joy and gratitude as "spiritual practices that are bound to a belief in human interconnectedness and a power greater than us."

I have always been a huge fan of gratitude practices, and I have had a devoted practice for over two decades; in fact, I attribute my family's ability to weather the devastation of Hurricane Harvey as well as we did to my practice. When I was in my late twenties, I began ending my day by thinking of one good thing that happened during the day—just one—and breathing a prayer of gratitude that it occurred. Often my "good thing" is relatively unimpressive, like noting that I uncharacteristically made my bed that morning and that it felt good getting into a made bed that night. But sometimes my "good thing" has been awesome, like stealing away from a less-than-exciting conference to go hot-air ballooning with a dear friend, or feeling thankful for that total stranger who appeared at our doorstep to muck out our house after the hurricane. In any event, what I've learned is that by developing a daily gratitude practice, I have, overall, become more joyful, simply because I stop to notice the things that are good.

What's true about our day-to-day lives is especially true when we devote our time to activism. Activism, at its core, is fraught with moments of conflict and pain and suffering. And while it's important to honor the difficult times and acknowledge that events were hard (even unimaginably horrible, in some cases), it's also important to give ourselves credit for keeping on keeping on. I mean, sometimes just waking up to face another day . . . well, there's *courage* in that. And that courage shouldn't be dismissed.

But it's also important, *especially* as activists, to embed joy and gratitude into our advocacy, particularly when things are going *well*. In fact, joy and gratitude are the most important practices to cultivate in order to establish longevity in our marches toward justice. And when we do it in community? Well, that's true celebration: gratitude and joy in spiritually uplifting, socially connected form.

Play evangelist Jeff Harry—he of the LEGO bow tie—is also a huge fan of celebration as a part of activism. "As a positive psychology coach yourself, Karen, you know the power to savor is crucial to a healthy mindset," he began. "And that's especially true in the chaotic world of activism, which can feel like such a never-ending struggle." He continued,

> In community organizing work, there is so much room for disappointment when fighting people in power, and there are so few wins. So it's crucial to celebrate each small win, especially if, as part of your activism, you're working with volunteers who aren't being paid. It's important to create games and be flexible with the ways you do outreach, to ensure that folks continue to have fun. It's important to shower volunteers with love and appreciation for what they've achieved. Volunteers are motivated by the progress and the ideals they're fighting for, so celebration of that progress and those ideals can make huge inroads in building a movement.

And then, to drive his point home: "When it comes to celebration, I think of the activists during the civil rights movement singing in jail after being arrested—they actually *celebrated*. The power to celebrate even under such extreme injustice is mind-boggling, but its purpose was also to intimidate powers who were trying to suck the life and joy out of the movement. Having fun and claiming joy can be such a revolutionary and rebellious act, especially in the face of massive injustice."

While Jeff didn't specifically mention John Lewis, the civil rights icon immediately came to mind. When Jeff and I spoke, Mr. Lewis had only recently passed away. Having grown up outside of the United States, I didn't know much about John Lewis's life until recently, when I really began to understand how truly important he was to the civil rights movement. I was duly awestruck whenever I saw his name.

John Lewis was born February 21, 1940, and grew up in poverty, the son of Alabama sharecroppers. His civil rights activism in the United States began when he was a university student, as one of the thirteen original Freedom Riders: a group of seven Black and six white young people who were determined to ride public transportation from Washington, DC, to New Orleans, at a time when it was illegal for Blacks and whites to ride on an integrated bus. He marched with Martin Luther King Jr. and gave an amazing speech at the 1963 March on Washington—the same huge event that included Dr. King's "I Have A Dream" speech—when he was only twenty-three years old. On what came to be known as Bloody Sunday in March 1965, as Lewis and other protesters crossed the Edmund Pettus Bridge in Selma, Alabama, a sea of Alabama state troopers descended upon them with billy clubs. A practitioner of nonviolence, Lewis never fought back, and he suffered a fractured skull in the fracas that followed. His assault was televised, and the ensuing outcry resulted in the passage of the Voting Rights Act of 1965, which prohibits racial discrimination in voting.

After he recovered, instead of quitting, Lewis served for thirty-three years in Congress. One of my favorite video clips of John Lewis was taken a few years ago, when he was dancing to Pharrell Williams's hit song "Happy." "This is my song," he said gleefully as he swayed to the music. "Nothing can bring me down." If anyone understood how to change the world without losing their joy, it was John Lewis.

So when Jeff mentioned the civil rights activists who were singing as they were arrested, I knew John Lewis had to be one of them. I was right. In his autobiography *Across That Bridge: Life Lessons and a*

Vision for Change, Lewis describes how celebration was actually a part of the strategy of the civil rights protesters. For the Freedom Riders, who were arrested for riding interstate buses in the segregated South, singing was a form of protest. He writes,

> Our strategy was to flood the penal system until it overflowed with Americans calling for justice. In the section where I was held, it was very hard to hear and impossible to see the other inmates, but it became clear that our strategy was working. Soon, the cells all around me were full of riders, and we began to sing songs of freedom to remind us of our purpose and keep our spirits high. . . . The songs seemed to aggravate prison officials who ultimately took away our Bibles, our toothbrushes, and even our mattress and bedding, leaving us to sleep on steel cots, all to snuff out the joy in our hearts. Parchman was a prison meant to break the hardest men, and the prison guards were frustrated that their worst punishment could not shake our faith. . . . Ultimately, we were released. I guess the state decided punishing us further was counterproductive.

In many ways, just as kindness is a form a resistance (as Asha Dornfest maintains), and joy is our birthright (according to actor Zuri Adele), so too is celebration. Celebration not only helps nurture the spirits of the individuals in our community; it cultivates a collective sense of joy and hope and optimism. And it can be the purest source of energy and determination to keep on keeping on.

Even though bringing joy to the work—and inviting people to celebrate with you—is one of the biggest secret ingredients to activism, it's also one of the most ignored ones. The more joy and celebration you can bring to your activism, the better you will feel and the more inspired others will be to join you. What elevates activism to a spiritual act is the instilling of meaning and joy in each experience.

Research, by the way, bears this out: the more you celebrate happy moments with someone else, the more joyful you become. And as we already know, a positive mindset can often be an indicator of future success. A study conducted by Dr. Robert A. Emmons of the University of California, Davis, and Dr. Michael E. McCullough of the University of Miami indicates that the more we celebrate and express gratitude, the higher the likelihood of making progress toward goals (not to mention the reduction of stress and anxiety). "A party without cake is just a meeting," Julia Child said. Celebration helps us cement the purpose and meaning in the work that we do.

And besides, it's just fun.

Brad Montague, the joyful creator of Kid President, has infused all aspects of his work with celebration, including a summer camp that he created with his wife. "The focus was on social good and service learning," he describes in *Becoming Better Grownups*. "Junior high and high school students from across the country would gather to celebrate the many ways they could make a positive difference in the world. Sessions were led by young change-makers who were leading projects in their communities. We got our hands dirty working together on things that needed addressed. Meals were packed and shipped across oceans. Benches were built and set up in our town. Good was spread."

Celebration, in other words, became the rocket fuel for his activism.

Even in situations where you're advocating for people enduring unspeakable horrors, joy and celebration can be a catalyst that activates others to help. This is the reason that I was so drawn to work with the ONE Campaign in the first place: their ethos has always been based on celebrating the good. I reached out to Ginny Wolfe, who used to be the senior director of strategic relationships for the ONE Campaign and the person responsible for my trips to Africa with ONE. I wanted to hear her thoughts on the reasons behind ONE's celebratory ethic. Now retired and living in Cambodia, Ginny was happy to share her insights with me.

"When you serve as advocates for people who live in extreme poverty, vulnerable to preventable, but deadly disease, there might , be an initial temptation to highlight the sad, the tragic, the horribleness that does exist," she wrote. "Showing the horrible might evoke pity—but pity isn't empowering. In fact, it's just the opposite."

In other words, joy might be a better strategy than tragedy for telling the story of activism. "We believed it's more respectful and productive to highlight and celebrate how a little bit of help can be a midwife to growth, security, and light," Ginny told me. "Having said that, to get to the joy, you have to do the serious studies and have the serious conversations that lead to national, even global policies. And then you have to show political leaders that the resources they allocate to critical programs actually work. Showing how they work gives power to people to help themselves, their communities, and ultimately, their countries. That's real cause for joy and celebration."

Jeff and Ginny were specifically speaking of working with volunteers and politicians, but celebration-as-motivation also works for employees of organizations focused on giving back. My friend Aimee Woodall, whose branding agency proudly declares their goal to be "activating people around things that matter," has embedded celebration into the company culture. As you may remember, Aimee's clientele is composed solely of nonprofits and civic-minded for-profits, so their successes actually help make the world a better place. And every Friday at 4:30 p.m., her entire team pops open a bottle of champagne to toast and celebrate all the successes—big and small—that her company has had during the week. They actually write their victories in a team journal to be sure there's a record of the good work they're doing. And of course, these weekly celebrations have the glorious side effect of embedding meaning into the work they do. This celebratory culture has resulted in her company's repeated appearance on Houston's Best Places to Work lists; but that's just icing on the cake. Used mindfully, celebration has been a tool to galvanize the people with whom Aimee is changing the world.

Finally, possibly the biggest reason that activists should cultivate a habit of gratitude and celebration: because we've earned it. I say this not out of self-congratulatory, pat-on-the-back egoism but rather as a simple fact. Any work that we do—whether it's in our day-to-day lives or when we're out changing the world—requires exertion and mindpower and persistence and courage. We need to learn to celebrate those commitments and labors as a matter of course. Understanding that we've been given the gift to, well, use our gifts, connects us with our purpose.

In his autobiography, John Lewis issues a call to action for each of us. He invites us to accept our nomination as lightmakers. "You are a light," Lewis writes. "You are *the* light. Never let anyone—any person or any force—dampen, dim or diminish your light. Study the path of others to make your way easier and more abundant. Lean toward the whispers of your own heart, discover the universal truth, and follow its dictates."

In other words, we are all called to join forces with others: people who shine bright and create light where there is darkness. We're called to lean into grounded yet unfettered optimism: understanding what constraints exist, fearlessly dreaming about what a better world looks like, and making determined strides to get there. We need to be unafraid to make some noise and get into "good trouble," as Congressman Lewis used to say—knowing that as long as that trouble is born out of love and light, we're on the side of right.

I hope you realize that although life can be difficult and dark, *you have the power within you to create light*. And together, as lightmakers, we can illuminate a brighter future for all of us now and for future generations on this planet.

EPILOGUE

LESSONS FROM THE BONFIRE

It was our final day of official meetings and site visits. Over the previous five days, we'd traveled all over Kenya: after meeting with Sam and Grace and other home healthcare workers in Kisumu, we'd visited maternal health workers, women and men who visit pregnant and immediate postpartum mothers to check up on them, making sure they are receiving adequate care and support. We had returned to Nairobi to visit a school founded by a church and parents of Mukuru, an informal community. From there, we visited Kibera, one of the largest informal communities in the world, to speak with staff of an NGO that provided a network of programs designed to advance health, education, ethnic cooperation, gender equality, and economic empowerment. A day later we were once again on the road, driving several hours outside of Nairobi to Nakuru to visit two farms: a dairy farm and a potato farm, both run by a collective of farmers.

At every one of these places, we were greeted with wide open arms: every single one of our visits began with our bus being met with enthusiastic song and dance, often with cries of *Karibu!* ("Welcome!") as we descended. Every official, healthcare worker, teacher, farmer, and elder who spoke with us over the previous five days did so with both deep knowledge of the issues at hand and profound pride in the advances being made in the health, both physical and financial, of their communities. And they shared their stories with warmth and kindness.

But on this last day, just like when we'd first landed in Nairobi, we were exhausted. We'd had site visits all day long, and on our final night in Kenya our bus was trundling its way from Nakuru toward Nairobi, with an overnight stop at a lodge located on a 150-acre reserve on Lake Naivasha, one that promised up-close views of gazelles, giraffes, zebras, and perhaps even a hippo or two. We'd have a bit of downtime before we began the twenty-four-hour trek back to the United States the following day; judging from the silence on the bus, we were all getting a jumpstart on that rest.

Suddenly, the silence was broken. "I know you're all tired," said Ginny, the ONE Campaign director and leader of our trip, "but we have a surprise waiting for you when we arrive."

Our driver negotiated the ninety-minute drive to the lodge, and when we arrived, we heard the now-familiar singing and music that we'd been hearing at every site visit. We were led to a lush garden where a feast had been laid out for our arrival. Someone handed me a gin and tonic. The setting was magical, and I took it all in, bobbing my head to the beat of the drummers who were performing their welcome.

Suddenly, I felt like I was being watched. I looked over and discovered Arthur, the head of our Kenyan team and our local guide, grinning at me. The two security guards who had accompanied us for the entire trip were with him, and they were all enjoying a beer. This was the first time I had seen any of them with an alcoholic beverage during the week; this being the last night of their assignment with us, they could finally relax. All three of them had been an indispensable part of our trip, and I'd spoken to each of them over the course of the week, learning about their families and lives.

I smiled at Arthur, and his grin grew wider. "Do you know how to dance?" he asked.

I started walking toward them. "I mean, before you asked that question, I would've said yes," I responded warily. "Now, I'm not so sure."

He laughed. "I'll teach you how to dance like a Kenyan. Here, let me show you this move."

At this, he began dancing, moving his body smoothly to the beat of the drums. "Come on!" he urged, inviting me to follow him. I began mimicking his moves, with what I assumed was all of the grace of the gazelles that frolicked in the grasslands surrounding the lodge.

Unfortunately, Arthur and his colleagues must have thought I danced more like a newborn giraffe. I caught them all stifling giggles. I stopped dancing, feigning offense. "You're *obviously* all laughing because you can't believe how *amazing* a dancer I am, right?" At this, they collapsed in helpless cackles. "Let's go, then; show me another!"

Arthur immediately shared another dance move, and his friends joined him. Again, I tried to copy them, and within minutes we were all laughing at how awkward I was. The four of us continued laughing and dancing, until we were finally interrupted and invited to join the huge buffet that had been set out for us.

Once we all had our plates, Ginny stood up and clinked a fork against her glass to get our attention again. We fell silent.

"It's been quite a week," she smiled. We cheered in response. "I want to thank you all for being here and working so hard to show the beauty and magic of Kenya. We hope you've been able to see the strength and determination of all of the doctors, health-care workers, NGOs, government officials, farmers, and so many others working toward Kenya's bright future." She spoke for a few minutes more, and invited her colleague Lauren to join her. Lauren had been responsible for all the details of the trip—sites we visited, and the itineraries for each day. She had also been responsible for watching the metrics of our journey: because of our collective writings on our various blogs and publications every night for the week, thousands of people had signed up to become members of ONE, committed to urging their government representatives to maintain or increase foreign aid to help fight extreme poverty and disease.

In other words, our trip was an unqualified success. We toasted in celebration.

By the time dinner was over, the temperature had dropped, leaving a notable chill in the air. I considered turning in for the night—it had been a long week. But one of our hosts called for our attention. "Please follow us," she said, when we'd quieted down. "We have something to share with you."

We all stood up and followed. She led us to a nearby hill, and there, at the top, was a huge bonfire, with logs placed around it for us to sit and relax. We all gasped with delight, and quickly found a spot to enjoy the warmth of the flames.

The bonfire set off bright sparks into the inky black sky. I sat there, mesmerized by the beauty of the flames, and felt incredibly peaceful. I was so grateful for the camaraderie that had developed among my travel companions and our new Kenyan friends. I reflected on the experiences of the previous week: meeting these amazing people, from doctors to activists, and marveled how interconnected we were. How, despite our differences, what resonated among us was bigger. I thought about the people outside of Kenya who had been following our words all week long. I marveled at what a privilege it was to be able to convey what we witnessed to such a wide audience while encouraging them to join in the fight against destitution. I knew that with that privilege came a huge responsibility: we owed the Kenyan people who had showed us such kindness a duty of care with the stories they'd shared.

I don't know exactly when I fully realized that I am an activist, but at the bonfire that night, I certainly grew far more confident in my own calling. I had joined in the labor to make a better world, determined to use my gifts to make the world a brighter place for others, and that made me a lightmaker. And as I sat with my travel companions and our Kenyan colleagues that evening, people whose backgrounds were so very different from my own, I became convinced that we were *all* lightmakers: it was possible for each of us to do our part, in all the diverse ways we could. We each had different gifts that we held in trusteeship, and we had become connected. Staring at the bonfire's flames, I thought of all the light we could collectively make.

Make no mistake: changing the world requires a considerable amount of focus and a hell of a lot of practice. Even if our activism isn't the sort that puts us at daily physical risk, the path is not easy. At times we'll look around and think: "The world is a Dumpster fire; I'm working so hard, and it seems to make no difference. Why do I even bother?" At times we'll get it wrong. Despite our good intentions, we'll make missteps, and some people will eagerly (and vociferously) point out where we've fallen short. We may even have to swallow our pride and make amends. Repeatedly.

But oh, there'll be amazing times too: times we will be able to see the progress we're making and the positive difference a change is having in someone's life. Days when there is tangible evidence that the environment is coming back, days when the bill will be passed, and days when the verdict gets handed down, ensuring the human rights of a marginalized group are protected. There will be moments when, because of our work, someone is finally listened to. There will be times of celebration, and of joy, and of deep, soul-felt gratitude. There will be times when all the work will be worth it. By embodying the lessons of both the activists who came before us and the lightmakers of our day, we can create a better world.

We can do this, my friends. There's no end to the light that we can make.

Author's note: The Lightmaker's Manual includes prompts to create your own spark statement or manifesto. I offer a Lightmaker's Manifesto on the next page to get you started, embodying the concepts discussed in this book. Feel free to adjust and amend to make it your own.

THE LIGHTMAKER'S MANIFESTO

I believe we are interconnected.
I believe peace is the true way for change.
I listen.
I honor my own inner wisdom.
I name my gifts, those which I hold in trusteeship,
knowing they are my superpowers.
My different is beautiful.
My privileges afford me the power to help those who are powerless.
When I fall, I rise, moving through any doubt I have in my abilities,
because I have evidence to suggest otherwise.
I am self-compassionate.
I love fiercely, and I refuse to succumb to hate, acrimony, or fury.
I believe joy, kindness, and celebration are acts of resistance.

I dream of a better world
and aspire to join in the march toward its attainment.

I blaze with courage and conviction.
I am called to action.
I am a lightmaker.

THE LIGHTMAKER'S MANUAL

JOURNAL PROMPTS, TEMPLATES, AND EXERCISES FOR
CULTIVATING A JOYFUL, LIGHT-FILLED ADVOCACY PRACTICE

JOURNAL ABOUT THE WHISPERS

One of the most revelatory things that you can do as you consider a life of activism is to begin a journal practice. Journaling can have far less structure than you're probably used to hearing about. In addition to using your journal to capture lofty thoughts, you can use it to capture ephemera: mundane tasks, random musings, and yes, sudden flashes of insight and inspiration. You can doodle in your journal, stick random cards and fortune-cookie fortunes in it, and use it to stash scraps of paper: seriously, it can be a catch-all of whatever is going on in your life. By treating your journal as something less than precious or literary, you may end up being inspired and making discoveries that you never would have considered. As a result, you may end up listening to the whispers that can bring you to the forms of activism that connect to your joy.

RULES

To cultivate a journaling practice, try journaling for twenty-one days, which is sort of the time-honored time frame for creating a habit. Over those twenty-one days, observe just two simple rules.

1. Don't rip any pages out of your journal. When you first start journaling, you may be tempted to rip out the pages that aren't perfect. Resist this temptation. Journaling is not about perfection; it's about capturing your thoughts or whims, however fleeting or random they might be. If the marks you've made on a particular page really bother you, then simply turn the page and start again on a blank one. If you make a mistake, or you doodle something you decide you don't like, or you don't think it's neat enough—heck, if someone's coffee cup leaves a stain on the open page—*it stays in the book.* This rule might be frustrating at first, but just trust me on this: for twenty-one days, do not rip out any pages. At some point you might return to the scribble, or even to the coffee stain, and be charmed by it. In fact, the annoying doodle may just hold the nugget of a great idea.

2. Keep your journal on you. Store it in your bag or your backpack. For the next twenty-one days, your journal should be your constant companion, easily accessible at a moment's notice. If you find yourself somewhere with a few spare moments, just whip out your journal to jot down your thoughts. You might even begin some of the other exercises in this book.

IDEAS

Those are the only rules. Pretty easy, right? As far as how to use your journal, I'd recommend the following.

1. Do "morning pages." Julia Cameron famously outlines this method in her book *The Artist's Way: A Spiritual Path to Higher Creativity.* Taking inspiration from her words, I'd suggest that first thing in the morning, you write at least two pages of whatever comes to your head: completely stream-of-consciousness writing, without any particular attention to spelling or grammar. You simply spill all the thoughts that are cluttering your mind. A tip: do your morning pages *before* you turn on your computer. In this way, you can be sure to focus on what's important to you for the day before your inbox rules your world. Your email should supplement what you want to accomplish for the day, not take it over.

2. Use your journal like a scratch pad. Keep your journal with you for the rest of the day and use the pages to follow your thoughts like a scratch pad. This idea—of using a journal as a place to keep random notes—may seem strange at first. Someone calls and leaves a message for your partner? Write it down in your journal. Need to make a grocery list? Into the journal it goes. Planning a trip? The packing list goes in the pages. Basically, for the next twenty-one days, anything that you would scratch on a piece of paper or even a napkin should happen in your journal. If you love color, use colored markers to highlight things that seem important. And don't get me started about doodling, writing down favorite quotations, or gluing in photographs or found postcards. Throw everything in there, with abandon. The beauty of this is that because your journal is chronological, you'll be able to easily find things—your notes, your ideas, your lists. This approach can be both a great way to organize life and an easy way to start "journaling" without feeling too exposed or weird about it.

PROMPTS

Because opening your journal for the first time can feel intimidating, here are a few journal prompts to help you get your practice started. These prompts will also help you begin thinking about your whisper. Simply pick one of these questions and write your responses, stream of consciousness, for at least two pages. The next morning, pick another and do the same, and so on. You may be surprised by where your inner sage leads you.

In this book, lightmakers Brad Montague, Jane Mosbacher Morris, and Mira Jacob shared some of the self-inquiries that help them make light, and their suggestions are included in this list. Feel free to use them as journal prompts as well, asking and responding to one each day.

1. What are the things I do that provide meaning and purpose to my life?
2. What things do I enjoy doing so much that, when I do them, I lose complete track of time?
3. What do I wish people would do to make the world better?
4. What realities in the world make me angry? What are the concepts that seem so obvious to me that most people never seem to understand?
5. Based on the answers above, what are things *I* could do to make the world better?

Brad Montague:
6. I wonder who needs help?
7. I wonder what they most need right now?

8. I wonder who might work with me to help them get what they need.

9. I wonder what the most wonderful thing could be that we all do together to help.

Jane Mosbacher Morris:

10. When I think about changing something about the world, what's within my full control?

11. When I think about changing something about the world, what do I have that's within my realm of influence?

Mira Jacob:

12. When I consider the "topography" of my life, where are the places that I'd like to explore?

SET DAILY INTENTIONS

One of the ways to ensure that you infuse your lightmaking work with meaning is by setting intentions at the start of every day. This involves answering three questions, inspired by Mallika Chopra (as discussed in chapter 8), making sure I remain healthy and connected and purposeful. So as you open your journal to do your writing for the day, consider the following questions and write a couple of sentences in response to them.

1. What will make me feel healthy today? This is an incredibly broad question, allowing you to answer freely, without constrictions. One day, hitting your home workout really hard might make you feel healthy, but on another day, just taking a leisurely walk might do the trick. On still another day, a twenty-minute disco nap might be in order. Or maybe drinking tons of water. Use this prompt as an invitation to tune into your body and your mind to see what they might need—from movement to meditation—and express that need in your journal pages.

2. What will make me feel connected today? This is about caring for your relationships. Maybe one day it means calling a family member to catch up. On another day, it might mean sending an email to a friend. Or doing something creative with or for someone. Take a minute to reflect on how you can feel connected to someone you love, admire, or respect.

3. What will give me a sense of purpose today? This might be my favorite of all the questions, because in essence, it calls on you to ask yourself: What can I do to make light? Perhaps on one day, you donate to a cause that's important to you. On another day, you might spend some focused time on a project that feels like it taps into your greater purpose. Again, the beauty of this question is that it allows you to stay on task but gives you the flexibility to alter what that looks like from day to day.

Include the answers to these questions in your journal, and then add their answers to your to-do list for the day. Hopefully this will inspire even more insights you can add to your daily journaling practice.

FIND YOUR LIGHT WORDS

Naming your own gifts can be challenging. Either your mind goes blank, and then you have nothing to say—or else it doesn't, and then you feel egotistical saying them out loud. But knowing what you're good at and what you love to do are key to determining how you can use these gifts to change the world. This exercise will help you name and codify those gifts so that you can plan your advocacy and activism in a way that brings you joy.

MAKE YOUR LOVE LIST

First, make a love list: an extensive list of things you love to do. Keep in mind that you are looking for *actions*—that is, a list of things you love *to do*, not just things you love. Because you'll end up using this list in many ways (creating a spark statement, for example, or adding to your daily to-do list), here's how I would suggest you do it. First, grab a cup of tea (or a glass of wine, or a cup of coffee, or whatever your poison), and get started.

If your journal doesn't have a margin, draw a line to create a considerable margin on the left side of the pages on which you're going to make your love list. Once you have made your margin, take about thirty minutes to make a list of everything you love to do on the right side of the margin. While you're writing your list, tell your gremlin of self-doubt to take a hike. Unless you're *incredibly* healthy, your gremlin is going to *love* poking at you during this exercise. Don't let it. This is one of those brainstorming exercises where *anything goes*: whether it's big or small, serious or silly. If something comes to mind that you know you enjoyed doing in the past, write it down. We want to get everything down that you can possibly think of that you enjoy. *Everything.*

Consider all areas of your life when you make this list. Think of your job and your hobbies. Your household and your life stage. Any recent achieved milestones and specific goals. For the purpose of this exercise, try to ignore divisions between different domains of life; instead, think of your life holistically.

To help you think about what to write down, here are some prompts:

- *What things do you enjoy about your current work?* How about your previous job or other obligations? How about your work before *that?*
- *What things do you enjoy doing on your time off?* Eating? Napping? Singing? Whistling? Drawing? Running? Making music? Whatever it is, it counts.
- *What are some of your favorite memories?* What were you doing during that time?
- *What hobby did you used to have that you never seem to find the time to do now?* Did you love knitting? Building bikes? Quilting? Painting? Reading? Add it to the list!
- *What did you love to do when you were a kid?* Even the silly stuff—like mud pies, or the Elmer's glue thing I mentioned from my list in chapter 4—counts.

Spend some time thinking about each of these questions, and as the answers come to mind, write them at the bottom of the list. Remember: you're coming up with a list of actions. This is an exercise that is best done when you have some time to answer the questions, so be sure to do this when you have some peace, even if it's an hour before you head off to bed. You're not going to want to short yourself on this one.

REVIEW YOUR LOVE LIST

Once you have made your love list, walk away from it for a while. Then come back to it over the course of a few days and add to the list if you remember something that you think needs to be included. The longer the list, the more you'll get from it.

Finally, when you think you've exhausted your list, go back through the items one by one, and ask yourself *why* you enjoy doing that thing. As you review each one, think about the best part about doing that item and how it makes you feel when you do it.

Once you have identified why you love to do the item on your list, add the reason as another item to the bottom of your list. For example:

- If you love playing the guitar because you love making beautiful music with your hands, then add, "I love making beautiful music with my hands" to your list.
- If you love cooking because you love creating a gathering place for your friends and family, then add "I love creating a gathering place for my friends and family" on your list.

Again, write these additional reasons as additional items on the list, in the form of an action or an activity. Your resulting list may seem repetitive, but hopefully the additions deepen the meaning of your earlier entries. Continue to do this for as many of the items on your love list as you can.

LOOK FOR PATTERNS

After you think you've thoroughly exhausted every item on your list, start looking for patterns. Some of the patterns may appear to be obvious to you, while others might require a bit of ruminating. If these patterns don't appear easily to you, don't worry; you're doing this right. Just take a deep breath. Also, if you can, set aside some time to do this exercise when you feel calm. Maybe go outside with your journal on your lunch break, or wait until you have a quiet moment in the evening. Then read through the items on your love list and notice if things seem related to you.

When you begin to see a pattern in the items, on the left side of your margin, make a notation about how several items relate. Write your categories as action words or action phrases. Some examples might be:

- connect
- visually stimulate
- make art
- analyze
- problem-solve
- do mathematics
- heal
- document
- move
- dance
- debate

Note that some items on your list might have more than one notation beside them, because they're indicative of several categories.

For example, for me, blogging is both visual and written expression, so it got assigned to both categories. This is totally fine.

CHOOSE THE TOP CATEGORIES

Once you have made your notations, start counting up the frequency with which each category appears. You may have at least two or three categories that show up multiple times in your margin, but you may have many more. Note the categories that occur most frequently and write them down in a separate list. Try not to write down more than five.

Now you should have one, two, three, four, or five words or phrases in front of you that describe the things that light you up. Congratulations! These are your light words. Write them down in your journal. Memorize them. Hold them close. These will be your guideposts going forward. And—wrap your mind around *this*—they might even be your superpowers. Even if you don't quite realize it yet.

NAME YOUR VALUES

Naming your core values may not be much easier than naming your gifts. Remember the story from chapter 6, about the exercise you can do with a partner in which you both name three heroes and then interview each other about why you chose those three?

While doing this exercise with someone else is empowering—having someone listen to you and then repeat back to you what you shared always is—you can glean just as much meaning from the exercise by doing this as a journal prompt. Here's how.

1. At the top of three clean, consecutive pages in your journal, write the names of three people you admire, one name at the top of each page. The three people you choose could be living or dead; real or fictional (Luke Skywalker, for example); someone you know in real life or someone famous.

2. Now, on the page under each of their names, write down every single thing you admire about each of them. Do this in a stream-of-consciousness way, listing as many admirable attributes that you can think of for each of them.

3. After you've written down all the ways that you can imagine to describe them, notice any patterns or trends. What attributes have showed up multiple times as you described the people on your list? What common traits do they display?

These attributes that you admire in others—the ones that keep showing up—are your core values. These are the values that will likely help you change the world.

COMPOSE YOUR SPARK STATEMENT

A spark statement is a declaration of what you want to be about. It is a personal mission statement: a summary of your call, your work, and your unique way of making light in the world. It represents the things to which you hope to hold yourself accountable, and it captures what you love to do, what lights you up, and what you hope that your work stands for. Your spark statement can be a powerful guide when making big decisions about life or activism or work.

After some serious soul-searching, I came up with this for my personal spark statement:

I believe in the interconnectedness of all who inhabit our planet.
I engage in the relentless pursuit of real, uncontrived beauty, in every form.
I illustrate that beauty is everywhere, even (and sometimes especially) in the most unlikely places.
In so doing, I work tirelessly to counter negativity, violence, discrimination, and desperation, and join forces with those who celebrate positivity, peace, kindness, and joy.
I convince the skeptical of their uncommon beauty, and I create tools to help the weary see the inherent power they hold in their own lives.
I provide hard, irrefutable evidence that there is good in the world, and I am fiercely dedicated to showing how beautiful our planet really is, one image at a time.

To write your own spark statement, answer the following prompts over the course of four or five days. Grab a pen and paper or your journal, and spend some time writing down your answers. You'll appreciate having them all in one place to reflect on as you write your spark statement.

- *Monday: What do I believe in?* This could be about your faith, but it could also be about your philosophies in life, parenting, leadership, and work. Think about what you believe your duty is as a citizen of the planet. What comes up?
- *Tuesday: How could or would I change the world?* If you could change the world, what would you do? What legacy would you like to leave after you've gone? How do you hope people describe you when you're not in the room?
- *Wednesday: What messages would I like people to receive from my work?* What do you want people to think about after they've experienced your work?
- *Thursday and Friday: Begin playing with your spark statement.* Grab your light words (from the work you did in the earlier prompts), your core values, as well as your answers to the journal prompts above. Start writing some sentences that encapsulate how you'll make the answers to your prompts a reality, using your light words. Think:

> I [CHANGE THE WORLD] by doing [A LIGHT WORD].
> I [TELL YOU MY MESSAGE] by doing [A LIGHT WORD].

Your spark statement doesn't have to strictly adhere to the template above—mine doesn't—but a template is a great way to get started. Massage it as you write it, until it feels right.

Also, please note that my statement is on the long side. Do not feel like you have to write pages and pages for your statement! Aim for five sentences, but more or less is fine—whatever captures who you are and who you aim to be. And I'd love to hear what you come up with. Be sure to check out my website at karenwalrond.com, and find the link entitled "Spark Statements;" you can submit your own spark statement and read what others have shared!

DRAW YOUR MIND MAP

Have you ever been faced with an issue on which you have tons of data? You know that you want to do something with the information, but you're not sure what. One of the most helpful and productive things you can do in this situation is create a *mind map*.

Say, for example, you've completed all the journaling prompts thus far. By now, you will have established your light words, identified your core values, and composed your spark statement. Drawing a mind map will help you integrate all this work. And since your spark statement is at the core of everything you do, you can build your mind map around this core statement. (A sample mind map can be found at the end of this section.)

First, open your journal (or use a large sheet of paper or your nearest whiteboard—whatever your pleasure). Write a summary of your spark statement—in bullet form, if that's helpful—in the middle of the page. Make sure to write this statement in the middle of your journal, page, or whiteboard, because you'll need a lot of space around it for brainstorming.

Once you've written your spark statement in the middle of your working page, add your light words around it. Link them to your spark statement by circling each of them with a different color marker.

Now we come to the fun part.

For each of your light words, ask yourself: *How can I make my spark statement become reality by doing each of my light words?*

As you think of ways to make that happen, write your ideas down *as fast as you can*, linking them to each light word. When I create my own mind map, for visual simplicity, I continue to use the colors associated with each branch of each light word, and then I just start writing down ways I can use my light words to make my spark statement a reality. Each time I come up with an idea, I put a cloud around it and link it to the appropriate light word in its associated color.

Make sense?

Keep in mind that not everything you write down should be something you know for a fact that you're actually going to do or are even excited about doing. For example, when I created my first mind map, the phrase "launch photography gallery shows" appeared on my map, and it wasn't something I was particularly keen on doing when I wrote it down. But I wrote it down anyway. The point is to capture *everything*. At no part in this exercise are you to rate which ideas are better and which are worse. It's about *spilling*: getting them all out as much as you can. Only later, after you've walked away from your mind map, or given it some thought, or added notes can you determine which crazy ideas are just that—crazy—and which crazy ideas are also brilliant ones.

Once you've exhausted all your ideas for using your light words to make your spark statement happen, then just jot down notes by each of them. These are your ideas about your ideas, or in other words: how you can make them happen. The notes could be how they relate to your core values, ideas that come up that don't seem very well thought out but might be interesting (I usually put a question mark next to those). These notes might even include thoughts about contacts you might have who might be good resources if you actually do decide to pursue an idea. Whatever. *Remember: this is just about spilling.*

And that's it. At the end of the process, you may not have figured out exactly what lightmaking work you're going to do. But you will likely have a better idea of the scope of what's possible, and perhaps a hunch about what to tackle next.

So let your mind map rest for a while. There's no need to figure out which idea is better than another—that is, until you're ready to create your star chart.

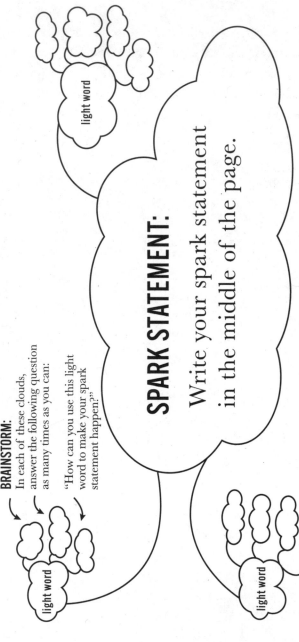

SPARK STATEMENT:

Write your spark statement in the middle of the page.

BRAINSTORM:
In each of these clouds, answer the following question as many times as you can:

"How can you use this light word to make your spark statement happen?"

light word

light word

light word

PLOT YOUR STAR CHART

Once you've created your mind map, you might notice that one (or more!) of the branches on your chart is crying out for your attention. Maybe it's a goal that will allow you to live in your purpose, align with your values, and work toward the change in the world that you've dreamed of. This goal might feel daunting. You may not really even know where to start.

It's time to plot your journey with a star chart.

To do this, you're going to need: 1) a flat surface—a posterboard or whiteboard is ideal, but your journal opened flat to two clean pages will do in a pinch; 2) your spark statement; 3) your mind map; and 4) some sticky notes. A sample template of a star chart is included at the end of this section; use it to help you understand the instructions below.

SPARK STATEMENT

First, at the top of your chart, write your spark statement. Again, your spark statement is the core of all the work that you do. Keep it visible as you work on your star chart.

WHAT'S MY GOAL?

Now grab your mind map and take a look at all the branches. Based on which branch seems to speak to you the loudest, pick a goal that you'd like to work on over the next year or so, but no more than two years. This should be a goal that you know will help you really live into your spark statement. It's best not to pick a goal that will require more than two years to accomplish, because circumstances—your own and the world's—can shift so greatly over that time period.

Write it down on the top left-hand side of your star chart, succinctly, in no more than two to three sentences.

WHY?

Next to your goal statement, answer the question: *What is my why?* In other words, consider all the reasons this goal is important to you, and make a list. Please note: your reasons don't have to be profound, but they have to be meaningful to you. As you make your list, be sure to refer back to your spark statement and your core values for inspiration.

WHAT DOES IT LOOK LIKE?

Finally, next to your why, answer this question, in list form: *How will I know when I have accomplished my goal?*

In other words, what will it look like? Are there metrics that need to be achieved? Certifications? An event or book or protest or fundraiser or project that you're organizing that will occur? How will you feel when you've accomplished it? What will others say about the result? Write down everything you can think of, in as much detail as possible. After this, draw your timeline, and then draw an arrow from your detailed goal description to the end of your timeline, dated with the future goal date/deadline by which you're hoping to achieve your goal.

Congratulations: you've just clarified your finish line!

WHAT'S IN MY GO-BAG?

Now it's time to detail what you have with you at the start of this journey. I like to describe this as your "go-bag": things that you already possess that provide evidence that you're already on your way toward your goal. This list will go at the beginning of your timeline, and might include:

- The education you already have that helps you access the knowledge you need to accomplish your goal
- People who will support your plan to change the world, either financially, through their participation, or even with their own knowledge and expertise
- Prior experience that indicates the goal is reasonable

And so on. Don't be afraid to list past evidence of perseverance, similar goals accomplished, or any documentation or memory that shows you that you can do hard things. List everything that you can think of that shows that you're already making strides, even before you make one conscious step toward your goal.

A note: As you do this step, don't skimp on time. Most of my clients tell me that this process—mindfully considering what they've already achieved that they can take with them toward their goals—is the most enlightening part of creating a star chart. Mining your past for your own successes is one of the best ways to cultivate confidence in your ability to tackle anything that lies ahead.

Once you've exhausted your list, draw a line from your list to the very beginning of your timeline, and put today's date. This indicates the very start of your journey.

MILESTONES

Now, having completed this go-bag list, put your timeline aside and grab your sticky notes. On each sticky note, *write one step that you'll need to accomplish in order to meet your goal.* Do not think of when you need to accomplish them right now, or how difficult any particular step might be to accomplish, or even whether or not you know how to do the step. Just think of what you need to do.

For example, if your goal is to start a nonprofit, you might want to write down on each sticky note things like:

- Come up with a name
- File for nonprofit status
- Design a logo
- Get a mailbox
- Find office space
- Find an accountant
- Connect with other nonprofit leaders in the area

Come up with as many steps as you can think of, and put each one on its own sticky note. Once you've listed all the steps you can think of, one per sticky note, come back to your star chart and place your sticky notes in chronological order in your timeline. Some sticky note events likely need to occur simultaneously. That's fine; they can overlap.

MILESTONE DEADLINES

Once you have placed your sticky notes, try to assign deadlines to each of the milestones on your timeline. You likely won't know how long some steps are going to take—especially those that involve other people and communities and movements. Give those steps pretty generous timelines, and maybe even highlight them by circling them. Add notes that indicate the things you might have to grapple with in order to accomplish the milestone. (For example: "How do I find a good accountant? Do I know anyone I can ask?"

might be a note that you'd add to the "find an accountant" sticky note, to remind yourself that you need to do a bit of research.)

After you complete this last step, your star chart is done—for now, at least. The point of the chart is to give you an overview of what lies ahead. In coming months, there might be changes and edits to the steps, new milestones added, or some milestones that become irrelevant and need to be removed. In any event, congratulate yourself for the work you've done to create a meaningful, reasonable goal—one that energizes you to take that first step on your journey.

> **Spark Statement:** The statement that encapsulates my values and what I want my legacy to be
> **What is my goal?** What I want to achieve
> **Why?** Why this goal is important to me
> **What does it look like?** What it will look like, in detail, when I accomplish my goal
> **What's in my go-bag?** What experiences, skills, talents, and education get you on your way

SPARK STATEMENT:
The statement that encapsulates my values and what I want my legacy to be

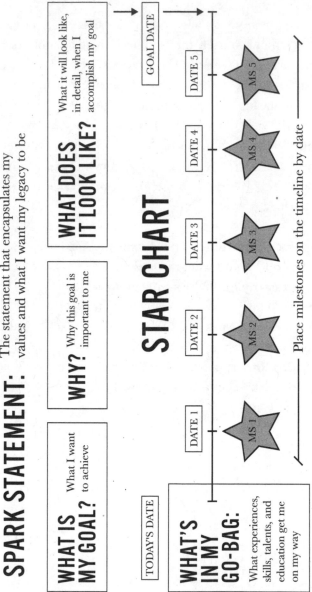

WHAT IS MY GOAL?
What I want to achieve

WHY?
Why this goal is important to me

WHAT DOES IT LOOK LIKE?
What it will look like, in detail, when I accomplish my goal

STAR CHART

TODAY'S DATE

WHAT'S IN MY GO-BAG:
What experiences, skills, talents, and education get me on my way

MS 1 — DATE 1

MS 2 — DATE 2

MS 3 — DATE 3

MS 4 — DATE 4

MS 5 — DATE 5

GOAL DATE

Place milestones on the timeline by date

CREATE YOUR SPIRE TRACKER

The daily intention-setting practice we learned earlier—in which you ask yourself three questions to set intentions for your daily to-do list—is forward-looking. It allows you to consider what you'd like to accomplish during the day before you actually set out to accomplish it.

Conversely, your SPIRE tracker, which you'll learn to create in this section, is a reflective tool. Based on the concept of "wholebeing," this tool provides a tracking method that encourages a couple of minutes of reflection every night.

To review, *wholebeing*, as defined by the Wholebeing Institute, is the term we use to describe what we consider fully holistic well-being, encompassing the following five elements:

Spiritual: leading a meaningful life and mindfully savoring the present

Physical: caring for the body and tapping into the mind-body connection

Intellectual: engaging in deep learning and opening to new experiences

Relational: nurturing a constructive relationship with self and others

Emotional: feeling all emotions, reaching toward resilience and optimism

To be clear, no one is expecting you to devote hours of your day to each of these areas of life every day. What makes for a holistic life is making sure you are attending to each of these spheres *over time*. And this is where a SPIRE tracker comes in.

I'm inviting you to begin a daily reflection practice, in addition to your daily intention practice. A SPIRE tracker is a simple way to track how many of the five elements of wholebeing you've paid attention to during the day. I've included a sample tracker at the end of this section for inspiration, but feel free to customize yours to capture your own SPIRE habits in ways that work for you. As you customize your own tracker, simply replace the titles of the bars with the types of the habits you want to track, making sure that the habits you're tracking over the course of the month correlate to the SPIRE method above.

Your habits could be daily, or weekly, or biweekly, or whatever—how often you actually practice them is entirely up to you. And as you think about what specific habits you'd like to do, don't forget to consider your star chart milestones, your light words, and even your spark statement for inspiration.

Here are some of the habits that could be included on your SPIRE tracker, as appropriate. Note that some of these habits could potentially be listed under several different categories.

Spiritual: Leading a Meaningful Life and Mindfully Savoring the Present

- Visiting your house of worship for weekly services
- Meditation
- Walking in nature
- Doing a gratitude practice
- Doing something meaningful and purposeful toward a milestone on your star chart

Physical: Caring for the Body and Tapping into the Mind-Body Connection

- Drinking a certain amount of water every day
- Working out

- Playing with your kids or your partner
- Playing with your pet
- Hiking
- Riding your bike instead of driving
- Hula-hooping (don't laugh: this is what I do!)

Intellectual: Engaging in Deep Learning and Opening to New Experiences

- Reading books (whether fiction or nonfiction—it all provides intellectual stimulation)
- Listening to podcasts
- Watching documentaries
- Doing research toward a specific goal on your star chart
- Taking an online course or pursuing a certification or a diploma
- Creating a website related to your activism
- Focusing on an editorial calendar for your online presence

Relational: Nurturing a Constructive Relationship with Self and Others

- Connecting with family and friends (even if it's just sending an email or text saying "I'm thinking of you")
- Sending a thank-you note or email in the mornings
- Revisiting your vision board, checking to see if you're living into it, and adjusting or adding as necessary

Emotional: Feeling All Emotions, Reaching toward Resilience and Optimism

- Reinvigorating your journaling practice, to express what you're feeling

- Taking a meditative walk to move through some "emotion tunnel"—using movement to help release stress
- Contacting a member of your star collective, or making an appointment for professional support (like a spiritual director or therapist or coach) if necessary
- Practicing self-compassion breaks as needed

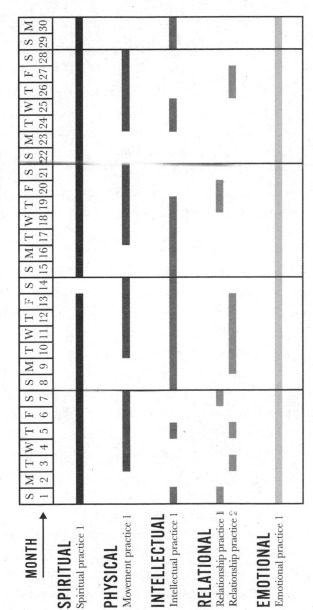

CREATE A LIVING VISION BOARD

Vision boards are a wonderful, tangible way to meditate on goals and dream about possibilities. When you focus on something in a tangible, hands-on way, your subconscious mind is engaged. Creating a vision board is a great way to begin working toward your goals.

Creating a vision board from scratch can be really fun, but please note: it requires a certain amount of focus and concentration, and it's not usually something that is done in a few minutes. It takes a bit of time. But the good news is that the process of creating a vision board can be meditative.

So I invite you to create a vision board that embodies what life would look like for you if you were to live into your spark statement.

First, gather as many of your favorite old magazines as you can—magazines that you don't mind cutting up or ripping apart. You can also include catalogs from favorite retailers, cards you've received in the past, anything that has lots of photography or other images that you love. Get as many different types of magazines as you can: magazines that relate to your hobbies, or travel, or fashion, or business, or social justice. The most important thing is to surround yourself with images that you love and that inspire you. If you don't have any magazines, sites like Pinterest can be a great source for images to print out and use on your board.

Then, with the question "What would it look like if I actualized my spark statement?" in the back of your mind, turn each page of the magazines, looking at all the photographs, illustrations, and headlines—each and every one of them, including the ads. Tear out (or print, if you're online) your favorites. As you look at the images, *don't be literal*. This is not an intellectual exercise, it's an *emotional* one.

Once you have all your images and words, it's time to make your vision board. Here's the thing about vision boards: they are essentially boards that have inspirational messages on them. Nothing more is required. There's no right or wrong way to arrange your images. It doesn't matter if you glue your images to a stretched canvas, poster board, manila folder, or just a journal opened flat. You can glue them in straight lines or haphazardly: whatever. It's entirely up to you.

In the past, I've used a stretched canvas for my vision board, but this year, I did something different. I used a cork board that I had lying around to create a *living* vision board: one that I add to and edit as I find more images and words that inspire me.

There are two schools of thought as to what to do with your vision board. One says that you should place a vision board in a prominent location where you can see it every day. The theory is that by placing it in plain sight, you regularly transmit the messages on the vision board to your subconscious brain, where they will subliminally work their magic. The second philosophy is the opposite: you're supposed to forget about your vision board altogether. In this view, the message transmission to your subconscious mind happened when you were hard at work making the board. According to this theory, it's the *forgetting* that works the magic—so much so that you can be surprised, down the road, to discover that an element from your vision board has come to fruition.

I've done both, and I can't necessarily say which one works best. This year, because I plan on adding to it periodically, I've hung my vision board in a corner of my home office where I can see it from my desk every day. Ultimately, however, after all this work you do to put it together, I'd hate to see you lose it. I'd place it somewhere where you can get to it easily and look at it. You might love what you've created and don't care if other people see it too; if that's you, hang it somewhere prominent. But if your vision board feels very private, you could hang it somewhere hidden, like in the back of your closet, so that no one but you can see it. If your vision board is static in nature, you might keep it inside a file cabinet near your desk, to pull out whenever you need to look at it (this works particularly well if you used that manila folder). Do whatever works for you.

ACKNOWLEDGMENTS

It's said that writing a book can be a lonely affair, but I can confirm that when writing a book like this one, the opposite is true. I am so grateful to so many people; without their unfettered generosity, this book would've never happened. They include:

My editor, Valerie Weaver-Zercher, who took a serious chance by contacting me out of the blue, saying that she was interested in a book about the intersection of joy and activism and thought I might be the person who could write it (and whose kind, straight-talking guidance helped ensure that I could do it).

My parents, Kermitt and Yvette Walrond, who read the book proposal and writing sample I composed in response to Valerie's inquiry, and both said, "Karen, you might be onto something"; also, my sister, Natalie Walrond, who has always been an enthusiastic cheerleader.

The ONE Campaign and Wholebeing Institute, two organizations whose work was formative in developing my deeply held belief in joyful activism.

The lightmakers, thought leaders, and activists who so graciously and generously shared their wisdom and light, including Aaron Billard, Aimee Woodall, Andrea Scher, Asha Dornfest, Brad Montague, Brené Brown, Ginny Wolfe, Jane Mosbacher Morris, Jeff Harry, Jess Weiner, Jesse Engle, Jordan Seaberry, Lauren Balog Wright, Mira Jacob, Sara Cress, Sean Fitzpatrick, Stephanie Wittels Wachs,

Tarana Burke, Terra Cothran, Valarie Kaur, and Zuri Adele. It gives me immeasurable hope and confidence that the world is in good hands with these luminaries.

Brenda Melvin, Cary Jamieson, Cheryl Newcomb, Christy Gray, Holly Tate, Kim Thompson, Lee Toepfer, and Susan Mann, generous, generous souls who helped me workshop the exercises included in these pages—their input and insights were invaluable. Also, Cathleen Falsani—without her early support of my writing, this book might never have been written.

My personal star collective and closest friends who, in addition to Asha and Brené, include A'Driane Nieves, Christine Koh, Jessica Ashley, Laura Mayes, Mark Savage, and Trish Haylon. Your continuous counsel and friendship always keep me from straying.

And last but not least, my Marcus and my Alexis: you are both the brightest lights in my life, and I love you.

NOTES

1. On Life-Changers and Lightmakers

12 **"I'm thinking less":** Erin Loechner, "My Own Ground Rules for Giving Holiday Gifts," *Design for Mankind: The Things We Keep and the Stories We Keep Close* (blog), November 21, 2017, https://designformankind.com/2017/11/holiday-gifts/.

2. On Joy, Meaning, and Surviving a Hurricane

23 **"It's wonderful to discover":** Dalai Lama [Tenzin Gyatso] and Desmond Tutu, *The Book of Joy: Lasting Happiness in a Changing World* (New York: Avery, 2016), 32.

25 **"well-being, contentment":** Martin E. P. Seligman and Mihaly Csikszentmihalyi, "Positive Psychology: An Introduction," *The American Psychologist* 55, no. 1 (2000): 5–14.

26 **"Your intelligence rises":** Shawn Achor, "The Happy Secret to Better Work," filmed May 2011 at TEDxBloomington, TED video, 12:05. http://www.ted.com/talks/shawn_achor_the_happy_secret_to_better_work.

27 **"There is nothing":** Viktor E. Frankl, Ilse Lasch, Harold S. Kushner, and William J. Wnislade, *Man's Search for Meaning* (Boston: Beacon Press, 2015), 77.

27 **"it only does so":** Frankl et al., *Man's Search for Meaning*, 79.

3. On Bangs, Whispers, and Trinidadian Rum

45 **"clarify our yearnings":** Julia Cameron, *The Miracle of Morning Pages: Everything You Always Wanted to Know about the Most Important Artist's Way Tool* (New York: Jeremy P. Tarcher/Putnam, 2013), loc. 83 of 710, Kindle.

45 **"scribbling his hopes":** Michael Scherer, "2012 Person of the Year: Barack Obama, the President," *Time*, December 19, 2012, https://poy.time.com/2012/12/19/person-of-the-year-barack-obama/.

46 **"In her Sikh Prayer":** Valarie Kaur, "'Breathe! Push!' Watch This Sikh Activist's Powerful Prayer for America," *Washington Post*, April 29, 2019, Perspective, https://www.washingtonpost.com/news/acts-of-faith/wp/2017/03/06/breathe-push-watch-this-sikh-activists-powerful-prayer-for-america/.

49 **"We should write":** Julia Cameron, *The Right to Write: An Invitation and Initiation into the Writing Life* (New York: Jeremy P. Tarcher/Putnam, 1999), 11.

5. On Integrity, Empathy, and Kindness as Resistance

66 **"Chookooloonks.com":** People always ask where the name of my blog, *Chookooloonks*, came from. It's actually a Trinidadian expression. We speak English in Trinidad, but this is a term of endearment, used especially when addressing a child, such as "Oh my goodness, you're such a sweet little *chookooloonks!*" It's just a fun little word we Trinis like to use for our kids, so it seemed pretty appropriate for my blog as we waited for the birth of our daughter.

69 **"Integrity is choosing courage":** Brené Brown, *Rising Strong: The Reckoning. The Rumble. The Revolution* (New York: Random House, 2015), 123.

74 **"I know that each time":** Dalai Lama [Tenzin Gyatso] and Desmond Tutu, *The Book of Joy: Lasting Happiness in a Changing World* (New York: Avery, 2016), 257.

79 **"Here's something I know":** George Saunders, *Congratulations, by the Way: Some Thoughts on Kindness* (New York: Random House, 2014).

83 **"When you show compassion":** Dalai Lama and Tutu, *The Book of Joy*, 293.

8. On Listening, Intentions, and Doing It for Fun's Sake

131 **"According to Brown":** Stuart L. Brown and Christopher C. Vaughan, *Play: How It Shapes the Brain, Opens the Imagination, and Invigorates the Soul* (New York: Avery, 2010), 17–18.

132 **"It is a critical fact":** Brown and Vaughan, *Play*, 126.

133 **"Play helps us":** Brené Brown, *The Gifts of Imperfection*, 10th anniversary ed. (New York: Random House, 2020), 128.

137 **"Play is called recreation":** Brown and Vaughan, *Play*, 127.

9. On Self-Compassion, Courage, and Aligning Your Star Collective

145 **"Yet according to the *Texas Tribune*":** Lilliana Byington, Brittany Brown, and Andrew Capps, "Black Americans Are Still Victims of Hate Crimes More Than Any Other Group," *Texas Tribune*, August 16, 2018, https://www.texastribune.org/2018/08/16/african-americans/.

150 **"Caring for myself":** Audre Lorde, *A Burst of Light: And Other Essays* (Mineola, NY: Dover Publications, 2017), 130.

151 **"According to the positive psychology research":** "SPIRE Well-Being," Wholebeing Institute, March 16, 2017, https://wholebeinginstitute.com/about/spire/.

153 **"According to Dr. Neff":** Kristin Neff, "Exercise 2: Self-Compassion Break," Self-Compassion, December 13, 2015, https://self-compassion.org/exercise-2-self-compassion-break/.

156 **"Brené Brown says":** Brown, *Rising Strong*, 245.

10. On Curiosity, Vision Boards, and Expecting to Fail

169 **"*Mister Rogers' Neighborhood*":** Brad Montague, *Becoming Better Grown-ups: Rediscovering What Matters and Remembering How to Fly* (New York: Avery, 2020), 140.

11. On Gratitude and Celebration

176 **"spiritual practices that are bound":** Brené Brown, *The Gifts of Imperfection: 10th Anniversary Edition: Including a New Creative Journaling Guide* (New York: Random House, 2020), p. 102.

180 **"Our strategy was to flood":** John Lewis, *Across That Bridge: Life Lessons and a Vision for Change* (New York: Hachette Books, 2016), 35.

181 **"A study conducted":** Robert A. Emmons and Michael E. McCullough, "Counting Blessings Versus Burdens: An Experimental Investigation of Gratitude and Subjective Well-Being in Daily Life," *Journal of Personality and Social Psychology* 84, no. 2 (2003), 377–89.

181 **"The focus was on social good":** Montague, *Becoming Better Grownups,* 97.

183 **"You are a light":** Lewis, *Across That Bridge, 207.*